PRAYER AND REMEMBRANCE

PRAYER AND REMEMBRANCE

REV. ROGER A. SWENSON

Foreword by Benedict J. Groeschel, CFR

AVE MARIA PRESS
Notre Dame, Indiana 46556

Scripture quotations used in this work taken from The New American Bible With Revised New Testament, Copyright © 1986 by the Confraternity of Christian Doctrine, Washington, D.C., are used with permission. All rights reserved.

Nihil Obstat: The Reverend Reginald R. Masterson, O.P.
            Censor

Imprimatur: The Most Reverend Philip M. Hannan
            Archbishop of New Orleans

Library of Congress Catalog Number: 88-82924

International Standard Book Number: 0-87793-396-0
                                    0-87793-395-2 (pbk.)

Cover photograph by Justin A. Soleta
Book Design: Elizabeth J. French

Printed and bound in the United States of America

To
Mr. and Mrs. Eugene McCahill

Contents

Foreword

This is not only a beautiful book on prayer, it is a book which teaches you how to use the ordinary things of life in a powerful form of prayer called contemplative meditation. It is a pleasure to recommend Father Swenson's work to anyone who, amid the pressing duties of ordinary life, feels the call to deeper prayer and does not know where to go to find it. Like all those who are convinced that there is a real possibility of higher forms of prayer outside the cloister walls for laity, active religious and clergy, I eagerly use and distribute works like this one as training tools for those seeking to grow in the spiritual life.

There are many roads to deeper prayer just as many streams can flow into the same valley. In recent years there has been much emphasis placed on turning within, on powerful states of recollection arising from centeredness. This method has proved helpful to many. But there is another method, that of prayer which is fed by the spontaneous and reverent consideration of God's action in all our experience, internal as well as external. Memory, emotion, knowledge and revelation all play a part in this prayer experience. I attempted to give a synopsis of this method in my own little book *Listening at Prayer* (Paulist Press, 1984). Father Swenson illustrates this same method effectively in *Prayer and Remembrance*. Weaving together some of the most powerful passages of Sacred Scripture with memories of his own religious experience, he gives the reader a series of templates or dynamic maps illustrating effective ways of using memory at prayer. His well-honed poetic sense makes these experiences come alive and makes his teaching both engaging and evocative. It is the essential quality of a fine writer that his or her experience evokes a powerful response of recognition in the reader. Father Swenson amply demonstrates this ability.

The painlessness of this teaching on prayer may accidentally lead the reader to assume that the method is in some way an inferior road to contemplative prayer. Most of those who are interested in prayer are drawn from the same personality types who believe that the best is always the most difficult. Leaving aside the fact that this is often true, it is clear in the case of the prayer of listening that the easier may be the most efficient. This kind of prayer focuses on the God-given potentials of the individuals. Memory, intelligence, freedom, imagination and emotion come together into a single white hot point of attention. The simple method of interior prayer taught by St. Teresa of Avila and illustrated in every legendary story about St. Francis is at least very similar to the technique of listening taught in this book. Only recently a Cistercian abbot in Ireland described contemplative prayer to me in very much the same way. In answer to a question about the method of prayer common to the monks, Dom Columcille of Roscrea described reading the scriptures, thinking about the message, fitting it into one's experience and raising one's heart to God. This is precisely the technique Father Swenson describes but not in the venue of the cloister but amid the scenes of ordinary life.

It is obvious that a book on interior prayer will not appeal to everyone, but Father Swenson proves it will be helpful, even genuinely exciting, to many who never thought they could experience interior prayer. If you want to pray, thoughtfully read this book a chapter at a time and you will find yourself drawing from your own memories and entering into a powerful experience of prayer. St. Augustine compares memory to a vast array of fields strewn with stones on which are carved the images of things gone by. He found much to pray about in the fields of memory when he linked these inscriptions to Sacred Scriptures. Father Swenson has done the same thing. So can you.

Fr. Benedict J. Groeschel, C.F.R.

The Solace of Nostalgia

Each of us travels along a trail of personal experiences that stretches back to the first moment of life in our mother's womb. Whether we like it or not, each of our yesterdays influences what we think, decide and do. True, we are men and women of free will, but our choices and the ways we exercise our freedom were shaped by people we met and situations we faced along the way. Each of us carries a picture of that trail, a road map of where we've been and how we were. Memory is the road map of our personal history.

Because the map of personal history is in daily use, it gets worn. Like the map in the glove compartment of your car, it has been unfolded, creased, refolded, ripped and misfolded. Age has faded the edges. Carelessness has added to the many stains and scribbles that make some portions indecipherable. As with the well-used road map, parts of our memories are no longer completely accessible. Some sections have been torn away; others, where highly colored fictions obscure the original data, are not to be trusted. Nevertheless, we continue to use the map of memory every day for we don't have the luxury of stopping at the next gas station to get a new one.

Although everyone relies on the power of recall, few are adept at using memory to nurture spiritual life. While we pride ourselves on being able to bring to mind ancient telephone numbers and well-hidden parking spots, such utilitarian appropriation of memories dulls this faculty for more sublime endeavors such as prayer. Because our memories are so fully engaged with numbers, names and nomenclature, we lose the sensitivity to nuance in remembrance. The clutter of "useful" items in our memories reflects rather accurately the clutter of "profitable" actions we must carry out each day in order to win the battles of modern life. Our memories become memory banks ingesting the reams of information required to survive in this busy world;

the better we can emulate the storage capacity of a computer, the better we shall be able to cope with the 22 challenges that will confront us this day. Unfortunately, we eventually stop remembering people, places and feelings and begin to enter data.

This book is not about bringing up dots on a display screen; it is about remembrance. Remembrance is more than merely calling to mind a byte of information; remembrance is the celebration of the past in order to enhance the present and define the future. This book is about prayer, about active, purposeful openness to God through the medium of memory. Prayer is a logical outgrowth of the God-given gift of memory and the life of memorable events through which you have lived. Some of these events were inspired by God; some were not. They are all valuable, each a medium for prayer. This book is about the Bible, itself a compendium of memories mostly about the past but some about the future. Here, biblical passages serve as stimuli to get you to unfold that worn map of personal history in order to see where and when God was working in your life. You will be surprised at his concern for the details.

Finally, this book is about nostalgia, which requires an explanation. Nostalgia has a bad press. Typically, a gathering of, say, old car aficionados will attract a cross section of people interested in automobiles of yesteryear. Each will have a different degree of affinity with Mercer Raceabouts, Stutz Bearcats, and Apperson Jackrabbits. Of course the newspaper reporter or the mini-cam will focus on the most outrageous of fanatics—the ones who eat and sleep old cars, the man who wears a straw boater to work, the woman who dons a duster for church. Invariably, they will speak of the ''good old days,'' not simply as a quieter time or a more peaceful age, but as the absolutely classic era, not only for automobiles but for life itself. There are more than enough of these antediluvians to keep the feature sections of the newspapers filled for years. They give frightening definition to the term ''nostalgia craze.''

Nostalgia is a poignant remembrance of another day, not a

12

craze or a fad or an industry. A person who dreams for a moment of a treasured insight or encounter is not a "nostalgia buff"; rather, he or she invites a memory into the dwelling of consciousness, there to entertain the sweet or bitter sense of time past, the feeling of gratitude or regret that accompanies the traveler as the milestones fade into the dusk. To be nostalgic is to be sensitive and tender with memories so as not to bruise them by exploitation. Nostalgia does not imprison remembrance, does not cage it for display to the public. Nostalgia listens and learns and lets go.

Memories are like fingerprints: No two have exactly the same configuration of whorls and creases. Yet, in sharing insights gleaned from our own personal history or from our observation of the actions of others, we find that no matter how different the situations we share a common humanity. The Bible is a good example of this principle. Our urban, motorized, techno-crazed lives couldn't be more different from the lives of nomads and exiles, shepherds and fishermen, citizens of empires and theocracies. Yet that collection of stories and sermons, which could be dubbed *The Book of Holy Memories,* is the world's greatest source of insight, inspiration and hope. We read it not because it reveals lifestyles strikingly parallel to our own but because it reveals a way of looking at ourselves and humanity that has changed little over thousands of years. That common essence is presented in colorful images and moving dramas. The result? The Bible as a book of memories captures our imagination, tames it, and teaches it the truth.

Whereas the Bible is divinely inspired, the present work is not. While each meditation flows from an evocative scripture passage, that flow has strictly human limitations. Pleasure or profit, insight or emotion will result from the invitation of the reader who calls into her or his consciousness the memory of a similar or, perhaps, opposite experience. The object of this book is not to fabricate memories for the amnesiac, but to stimulate remembrance for the reflective Christian.

13

Remembrance, here, is not an end in itself, but a vehicle for knowing better the intimate presence of God. There is no simpler method of praying than activating the memory of God moving in your life. These meditations step back from the highly structured practices of prayer that cry out to Christians from thousands of bookshelves and cassette players. Those methods may work wonders for some, but they strike many others as much too complicated for communion with Perfect Simplicity. Memory, the faculty of remembering, is radically simple, the incarnation of a divine attribute given to women and men. Should the gift not then be used to discover the giver?

When it comes to prayer and remembrance, there are no empty memories. Even the darkest recollection can prompt one to praise God. Think, for example, of the living memory of the Holocaust. Some wonder why Jewish people continually rehearse a tragedy that brought death to millions. Surely, many of the survivors and their kin will tell you that theirs is a preventive memory. Only by keeping the horror alive will they insure that it will not be repeated. The devout Jew will agree, but he or she will also tell you that God was present and active and alive among the dying in Auschwitz and Treblinka and Bergen-Belsen. They treasure the memories of his mercy in the midst of madness. The fact that you and I may like to forget sorrow doesn't mean God forgets the sorrowing. You will find in these pages some dark remembrances. These memories, as much as those of happier times, reveal the work of God. His compassion is well worth prayer.

Since your author admits to an age somewhat to the west of his prime, a valid question arises. How old does one have to be to engage in the kind of prayer that flows from nostalgia? You don't have to be "of an age" to profit from this book, but you should be "of a mind" to let another guide you along the road map of common experience. Much more brings us together than separates us. Chief among these commonalities is our shared desire for union with the Lord in prayer.

These meditations are meant to encourage prayerful reflection on how God once acted and is now acting in your life. Each meditation is divided into four parts: scripture, reminiscence, application to prayer and prayer itself. Each remembrance finds its inspiration in the preceding biblical passage. Read the scripture slowly. If you experience God drawing you to himself at this time, do not feel obliged to press on immediately. Enjoy this intimacy with the Author of the Holy Word. When you do begin to read the remembrance, let it breathe. Don't get bogged down in minutiae; don't attempt to match each detail with a similar experience in your own life. Nostalgia is not a science; it is a very unscientific gathering of feelings, insights, longings. The people and the scenes that enter your consciousness will now serve you by leading you closer to the Creator of memory. God's creation must lead to God. The third part of each meditation is a practical guide to one way of prayerful communion with God. Again, let yourself be carried away from details that did not square with your experience. See the final prayer-poem as one man's path through memory to the Father of memories. For you, for today, it may be the only conclusion possible. It might be an aid for those who come up dry. Aridity falls upon even those most devoted to prayer. No matter how you use these meditations, keep in mind that the object of each one is union with our loving Lord. Memory is the means; God is the end.

The solace of nostalgia is the consolation we experience when remembrance results in prayer. We do not trek back into the past to heal dark memories. Rather, we call forth memories dark and light to serve as catalysts of consolation in the present struggle. Through our tender recollection, God speaks his holy words of peace and hope and forgiveness, those qualities now in his holiest Word, Jesus, the Christ. Ah, yes! We remember him well.

R. A. S.

That Perfect Day

While the crowd was pressing in on Jesus and listening to the word of God, he was standing by the Lake of Gennesaret. He saw two boats there alongside the lake; the fishermen had disembarked and were washing their nets. Getting into one of the boats, the one belonging to Simon, he asked him to put out a short distance from the shore. Then he sat down and taught the crowds from the boat. After he had finished speaking, he said to Simon, "Put out into deep water and lower your nets for a catch." Simon said in reply, "Master, we have worked hard all night and have caught nothing, but at your command I will lower the nets." When they had done this, they caught a great number of fish and their nets were tearing. They signaled to their partners in the other boat to come to help them. They came and filled both boats so that they were in danger of sinking. When Simon Peter saw this, he fell at the knees of Jesus and said, "Depart from me, LORD, for I am a sinful man." For astonishment at the catch of fish they had made seized him and all those with him, and likewise James and John, the sons of Zebedee, who were partners of Simon. Jesus said to Simon, "Do not be afraid; from now on you will be catching men." When they brought their boats to the shore, they left everything and followed him (Lk 5:1-11).

It was one of those days when you hoped the bobber would never bob and no impertinent perch would accept the invitation wriggling on your hook. The rhythm of the gentle play of the waves against the side of your little boat pulled you deep into yourself. It wasn't sleep but the opposite of sleep that whispered under the bright sun; it was awareness. The lake became your universe, each feature of the shoreline now crystal clear in your vision. You were no longer part of the scene, no longer subject to the light breeze and the warm rays; now you were master of this world, commanding this tree and that precipice to stand out from the background for your inspection.

Think back on what you saw that day. It was more than water and woods and sky. It was the grandeur of God, a world less than a mile in diameter, cupped in his mighty hand, and offered to you. The lap of the water against your lazy boat was the beat of God's heart, the cry of the loon his voice, the wind his will. And all for you, to please you and make you sigh in wonder at the goodness of the giver.

Surprising details come floating back: The boat's worn oarlocks, smooth and shiny from hundreds of circuits of this tiny universe; the great pines insistently pointing to their maker; here and there the gray husk of a tree that had caught his lightning; the lake itself, smooth as glass and then rippled by divine will; the half-submerged log with the wary turtle waiting for your next move; suffusing all, the stillness.

The call of this memory is in the stillness of that afternoon. Yes, flies were buzzing, waves lapping, birds arguing, but it was so still. . . . Someone had commanded quiet in the midst of the routine noises of your little world. You were still, making yourself sensitive to the slightest sensation, allowing yourself to be vulnerable to the most delicate change in the air, for you knew that here God was speaking to you.

Like Simon and his companions, you had gone out to fish, though without commercial ambition. Like the men in the gospel, you had caught nothing, a blessing only to you. Like them, you returned to shore changed.

For the fishermen on Lake Gennesaret, a new world was born. Suddenly, in the face of a fisherman's idea of heaven, a net-breaking catch, fishing didn't seem quite that important anymore. So overcome were they at the power manifested in this new preacher that they dropped everything to follow him. God had spoken to them in a moment of nature's perfection. Whoever this rabbi was, he had the power to make the world perfect for a little while.

God taught you the same lesson on your lake of memory. He has the power to make your world perfect. The buoyant breeze, the warm sun, the playful waves were his perfect gifts to you. On other days, he had given the best wine to the members of a wedding party, new skin to a leper, clear vision to a blind man, renewed life to a widow's son, a miraculous catch to some fishermen. And on one special Sunday morning he gave eternal life to a dying world. The day on the lake was as perfect for you as the leper's day, the blind man's day, the Lord's day. Neither you nor the fishermen on Gennesaret could have asked for anything more. Yet, your gifts seemed exactly opposite. Their nets broke; you caught nothing.

In his wisdom, our heavenly Father knows all men and women want the same thing, but have widely differing expectations about the form this gift should take. We all want God. We see God, however, in various manifestations: love, prosperity, health. The fishermen saw God in the abundant catch. He gave himself to them in a way they could understand. So much did they appreciate his self-manifestation that they were willing to do his messenger's bidding immediately. So completely had their perceptions changed that they were ready to give up that world touched by a divine sign in exchange for the mysterious vocation to which that sign called them.

On your lake, God gave himself to you in a world undisturbed even by a fish tugging on the line. You saw with a new clarity his goodness in nature's perfection. As with the fishermen, he manifested himself for a purpose. He was calling you to a new world. You may still be unaware of the dimensions and characteristics of that new world. The fishermen left their nets and began to live a different life that very day. Your life probably did not undergo such a dramatic change when you pulled your

19

boat ashore. But God's more gradual approach with you does not mean your work is any less important than that to which he called the first apostles.

"The LORD gave and the LORD has taken away; / blessed be the name of the LORD" (Job 1:21). He took away the fishermen's perfect world and gave them trial, terror and finally triumph. To you, so long ago, he gave a perfect world of clarity and awareness that lasted only until the prow of your little boat touched shore. You thought the decision to leave the lake was yours, but in reality God took it from you. Had it been in your power, you would have returned again and again in a futile attempt to feel his breath in the soft breeze. Instead, God began to reveal to you a new world, perhaps one with its share of trial and tears. But you can return to that moment on the lake in memory. It was such a perfect day, such a perfect gift. The memory of the day your Father in heaven unveiled his face will be your strength and hope as you gradually discern the latitude and longitude of this new world.

Perfect prayer is prayer with no strings attached, the prayer of Jesus in Gethsemane, "Not my will but yours be done" (Lk 22:42). A soul seeks release from the coils of self preservation, from knots of egocentricity, in order to be given over to the work of the Father. To accommodate this yearning, the praying person must make a sometimes difficult adjustment in routine and relationships to achieve harmony with the beat of God's heart. Most important, perfect prayer is approached without any expectations; its single object is conformity with God's will.

Most of us can count our experiences of perfect prayer on the fingers of one hand. The duties and surprises of everyday life conspire to steal the time, tarnish the intention, sunder the silence. But still we try, for we know that the demands of family, job and Christian mission must take second place to seeking spiritual nourishment. Without prayer these needs could not be met. Aware of the absolute necessity of regular prayer, we structure each day to provide the time to renew our resolution and listen for the voice of the dove. At least this is the way life would unfold in the best of all possible worlds. Unfortunately, most of us do not live in that zip code.

The pace of modern life seldom allows the opportunity to find that placid lake or golden meadow or windless precipice where the ancient masters of contemplation met God. More often, we plop on our complaining knees in a bedroom that needs dusting while the noise of traffic in the street competes with canned laughter from the television downstairs. Yet, because of the memory of a treasured walk in a forest or a visit to a country church, we can at least approximate the rhythm of perfect prayer. We can slow down and let our minds grow quiet because the stillness was part of that golden day when we achieved communion with the Lord without really trying. The traces of that effortless encounter—the serenity, the palpable presence of divine love—still linger whenever we try to pray. The world stopped for a while and we were able to catch the Spirit on the wing.

God offers you the same Spirit today amid the clatter and distraction of daily prayer. He reminds you of that time at the lake when you were sure you heard a call. The whole world seemed poised for transformation; the only barrier to a glorious future was the horizon, and that would fall away as soon as you rose. You were suffused with a feeling of impending rebirth, the offer of a mission waiting just over the rim of the earth. But you were too attached to what you knew, too much in love with what you could hold in your hands. Having come to perfect prayer, you couldn't hold on to it and the world at the same time. That prayer still sings to you beneath the beat of a busy street. It is the low murmur of a dove calling you once more to pierce the mystery of God.

21

LORD,
I would be still this day,
at rest in a world cupped in your hands.
Yet even while fleeing the throb of trade's traffic
I cannot damp the inner pulse of acquisition,
    forgetting that having been given,
        I need not strive to get.

Having been given stars in stately arches,
    the earth solid yet soft enough to cradle my fate,
    a yellow sun benevolent not blazing;
having been given lips to praise you,
    a spirit to seek you,
    a heart to welcome you,
I must not ask for more,
    for more would gild the lily,
        tint this fragile moment with care
        for ownership and preservation.

Gentle me, LORD,
    gentle my impatience for results;
    make my grab a futile grasp.
    Let
        me
          let
            go.

Soft the Spirit you breathe upon my prayer,
    soft upon sharp expectations
    made malleable in your hands.
I hear in the rustling of leaves
    and rippling of waves
that pristine invitation
    echoing from Gennesaret,
    a call to contemplate the face of God in serenity.

Save me, LORD,
    from saving myself
        from what is truly new:
            the untested
                    unfettered
            ineffable
                        unvarnished
            unharnessed revelation of God's tomorrow.

Can there be any moment but this—
    perfection between tick and tock,
    a glint of glory red and gold upon your palm?

LORD, prison me within that chaliced world.
    I would be still this day.
        I would be blinded by the light.
        I would be yours.
            Amen.

Driven Snow

He sprinkles the snow like fluttering birds;
    it comes to settle like swarms of locusts.
Its shining whiteness blinds the eyes.
    the mind is baffled by its steady fall.
He scatters frost like so much salt;
    it shines like blossoms on the thornbush.
Cold northern blasts he sends
    that turn the ponds to lumps of ice.
He freezes over every body of water,
    and clothes each pool with a coat of mail
    (Sir 43:18- 21).

The first flakes fell in the late afternoon. So gray was the sky, so few the flakes that you couldn't prove it was happening, only sense it, take it on faith. Only the sidewalks knew for sure; they told the secret on their flat, honest faces now stippled with moisture. But even these concrete criers would not divulge the dimensions of the snowfall. Flurries and blizzards began the same way.

The day weakened and died. It had not the heart to wait for the next report. Shortly after 6:00 p.m., some atmospheric discontent caused the flakes to grow. They became heavy and wet and fell like marshmallows past the kitchen window. The kids hurried through the vegetables and out the door to taste the frozen confections on their tongues. A sodden blanket was forming on roofs, cars and shrubbery. Too soon yet for snowballs. With the radio still talking about flurries, you decided to make a trip to the store and added flashlight batteries to the list. Two blocks from the house, you could see what it was going to be. The wind was picking up, the tires were crunching on an inch of snow, the radio finally spoke of blizzard conditions to the west. At the store

25

you discovered that once again you had forgotten the list, but you remembered the batteries. On the way home, you saw Mrs. Harmon's old Ford in front of her place looking now like one of those streamlined "step-down" Hudsons, so much had the accumulation of snow transfigured it.

The wind scoured the walk between the garage and the house. Around the corner of the back porch a drift was building. The kids weren't playing in the snow; they were standing still, making themselves vulnerable to the steady force hinting of fury to come. Like dogs and deer, they felt the need for ready haven. They were glad you were home and that filled you with a familial affection you hadn't felt in a long time. None of them protested your measured suggestion to come in. But now the radio was reporting a marked decrease in the wind and snow to the west. Soon it would stop here, too, with an expected accumulation of four inches. Even though the wind was as strong as ever and the shed at the bottom of the back yard was totally obscured by a solid curtain of white, you were no longer prisoners of the storm. Six-sixteen Maple was not cut off from the creamery or the butcher shop. The power lines would not snap tonight; the plows would be out before daybreak. You would not be silently beseeched to show doughty endurance by a family huddled in chilly terror.

The kids didn't even bother to see how it came out. The ten o'clock news said no schools would be closed, all roads opened by 5:00 a.m., depth of snow from two to four inches, highest winds, 35 mph, some drifting on secondary roads. A little after eleven, when everyone else was asleep, you pulled on your overshoes, donned your parka, and went out to chart a brave new world.

The sky was quite clear; a few winter stars stood off and blinked in disinterest. The feisty wind had been replaced by crisp, still air. Your footprints were the first on this virgin earth; the sound of boots the first sign that this new world would know a master. You set off like Peary for the Pole to see a land reformed through good intention, a place where irregularity was evened and smoothed by the wind's chisel and trowel, where the garish colors of decay were covered with the baptismal robe of purity, a place where the roar of contention was muffled, muted and finally silenced beneath the weight of awe.

God "sprinkles the snow like fluttering birds" to give us a taste of what our world would be like if good intentions ruled. The poor man's hovel and the rich widow's mansion would take the same shape, command the same view, and indiscriminately welcome those who seek rest and refreshment. The angular projections of our cities, mirroring the thrust and parry of trade, would give way to the ample curve of solace and mutual concern. Men and women walking through the storm would wear the robes of the Apocalypse and become the elders and saints around the heavenly altar. Traffic would slow and stop, horns and sirens fall silent. In the world of good intentions, there would be no competition for right of way, no need to conquer one's destination by brute force. The pure of heart would hold serene, if fleeting, dominion.

The sun will return and with it reality. "At noon it seethes the surface of the earth, and who can bear its fiery heat" (Sir 43:3). Good intentions are so evanescent even God cannot preserve them when they fall into the hands of fools. The blazing, nuclear furnace of pride, the sun of injustice, rises every day to melt the dream of amity, equality and parity. You walked through your pristine world for perhaps an hour that night. You were there precisely because you knew how impermanent the spectacle would be. In truth, your boots brought the first bruises of decay as they punched down to the raw gravel and brown grass. You were Adam whose footprints were pride. You were Eve whose ardor for self melted all good intention. Yet in spite of the mud in your wake, you tramped on through the white Garden, unable to turn away from what could be.

Too often our prayers are precious miniatures, the controlled yearnings of Christian sophisticates. We suppose that a petition for a return to harmony in the lunch room is more apt to get results than a plea to relieve religious oppression in the Soviet Union; we feel that way because we have our parts to play in the lunch room, but will never set foot in Russia. That our good intentions are often much more parochial than global betrays a lack of faith—first, in God's infinite power and will to save; second, in the power of the purity of the human heart, that single-minded resolve Jesus praised in the sermon on the mountainside. He would have us go to prayer with wide horizons and abundant optimism.

It takes an authentic act of will to fight the feeling of isolation that shrivels the good intentions of the person who prays in solitude. If prayer is loving, trusting communion with God, then by the very nature of its object, prayer is cosmic. Your prayer-place, that circle of attentiveness you enter with the highest purposes, becomes part of the dynamic of love that links the resentment of South African blacks, the shifting allegiances of the American electorate, the most private thoughts of prime ministers and popes, the insight of the cancer researcher, and the inattention of the little boy down the street playing with matches. Like St. Therese of Lisieux, who became co-patron of foreign missionaries without ever leaving her convent, we should go to our quiet rooms expecting the walls to open to the world.

There are too many misers on their knees, counting out precious moments on special, personal, private, secret, selfish requests that their cocoons might be a little softer. They forget that God knows the difference between what they think they need and what they really need. What many of us really need is to learn to pray with a world-view. To achieve this wider horizon in our prayers requires a quest for purity of heart, that is, a surrender to God of all anxieties about our own well-being, in order to gain the perspective necessary to seek the renewal of the face of the earth.

God wants our expressions of interest in and support for his efforts to transform the scourges of racism, tyranny, terrorism and poverty. He wants to hear the evidence of our loving intention that good may triumph, for that is his intention also, and he is honored by those who conform their wills to his. Prayers for universal peace and justice, healing and compassion in places far removed from our comfortable surroundings let God know that we wish to share his concept of redeemed humanity. While we may not be sure whether he wants us to get that promotion at the office or that bingo jackpot, we can be certain that mutual understanding in the Middle-East is God's purpose.

Align yourself with God's highest purposes whenever you pray. With all the confidence you can muster in this cynical world, ask that a mantle of renewal might be draped over this wounded world, a world that you too have scarred with pride and trampled with selfishness. Once you've admitted your sins, you need not linger over your tracks. Look ahead in prayer to see the shapes of new dreams across the wide horizon of humankind's hopes. They are your hopes. They are God's hopes. Make his intentions yours.

Miryam of Nazareth,
small-town girl with urgent dreams,
taut thread
in the warp of a tattered remnant,
you dared to weave a mantle
spun from ancient longings
and with it cloak the earth
in hope.
Intercede for me,
that I may put on the new man.

Mary of Bethlehem,
trudging to confinement in a stable,
bearing the idea of salvation
beyond the pale among the stars
you brought into the wilderness
a light
revealing graceful shapes
within the darkness.
Intercede for me,
that I may brighten the world with love.

Mother of God,
chanting in the silence of the cosmos
songs learned long ago
in Galilee
now become the universal anthems
echoing the will of God,
transforming worlds and galaxies
and hearts,
intercede for me,
that I may sing the new creation.
Amen.

The Powerhouse

Jacob departed from Beer-sheba and proceeded toward Haran. When he came upon a certain shrine, as the sun had already set, he stopped there for the night. Taking one of the stones at the shrine, he put it under his head and lay down to sleep at that spot. Then he had a dream: a stairway rested on the ground, with its top reaching to the heavens; and God's messengers were going up and down on it. And there was the LORD standing beside him and saying: "I, the LORD, am the God of your forefather Abraham and the God of Isaac; the land on which you are lying I will give to you and your descendants. These shall be as plentiful as the dust of the earth, and through them you shall spread out east and west, north and south. In you and your descendants all the nations of the earth shall find blessing. Know that I am with you; I will protect you wherever you go, and bring you back to this land. I will never leave you until I have done what I promised you."

When Jacob awoke from his sleep, he exclaimed, "Truly, the LORD is in this spot, although I did not know it!" In solemn wonder he cried out: "How awesome is this shrine! This is nothing else but an abode of God, and that is the gateway to heaven!" Early the next morning Jacob took the stone that he had put under his head, set it up as a memorial stone, and poured oil on top of it. He called the site Bethel, whereas the former name of the town had been Luz (Gen 28:10-19).

The old lady with the beads finished her last Glory Be and fell into the idiosyncratic rhythms of her recessional hymn. It was announced by the discreet sound of a kiss upon the tiny crucifix. Then, a sharp clatter as she dragged the rosary across the top of the pew and into her purse, which closed with a soft click. She stood up slowly, an arpeggio of snaps and cracks issuing from her joints. The kneeler came upright with a hearty boom. The coda was all shuffling and sighing receding to the vestibule. Her hand dipped in holy water made no sound. This rest was followed by an abrupt groan as she pushed against the heavy door. It closed behind her with a gentle whisper. Her recital was over until tomorrow.

How good it was to be alone once more in the parish church, your private chapel until someone else decided this late summer afternoon to ponder the imponderables. Not that you were the master. Rather you had come here to be mastered, to be led to the truth in a confusing situation, to be guided to wisdom as you sought to discern the Lord's will. Time has obscured the precise reason you tarried that day, but nothing can erase the memory of how that church looked and sounded. It was not your first visit by any means; your sense of tenancy stemmed from a kind of squatter's right, shared, of course, with the old diva of departures.

As always, you had arrived before the light that streamed from the west windows crept across the terrazzo of the center aisle. You laughed at the superstition that in the time it took the varicolored beams to completely cover the floor your prayer would be answered. You tempered this presumption by admitting that most often the answer would remain unknown to you for some time, perhaps forever; still you knew it was a dangerous game you were playing, testing God. The silent tide of refracted sunlight was the only movement in this empty chamber, the only intimation of God's dynamism and power. The delicately carved frets on the ends of the pews never changed; the mahogany crosses wrapped with vines and clusters of grapes stolidly assumed their duty of keeping young and old alike from falling into the aisle. On this quiet day, the baroque lamps hung from the high ceiling as immobile as if they were suspended on lead

32

pipes. Jesus pointed stiffly to his sacred heart, Mary's rosary was cast in pewter. Even the tiny flames of the votive lights stood stock still. The whole church held its breath as the bands of red and green and blue moved over the terrazzo.

You were in your favorite spot, right between "In Memory of Patrick Murphy" and "Our Lady's Sodality." The former, a window now in shadow, portrayed St. Francis of Assisi receiving the stigmata with thin red rays piercing his alabaster skin. The latter showed St. Therese, the Little Flower, ablaze in the summer sun, as if God's glory were shining through her meekness. Your place was well forward of the center of the church, far enough from the old lady so that her mumbling would disturb you only a bit, close enough to the crucifix to number the ribs. This was your place where you came to be molded, a little church like many others, brick and stone on the outside, good oak pews and mahogany bas-reliefs on the inside, a gingerbread altar of niches and crannies harboring plaster angels, a tabernacle hidden behind a curtain of gauzy gold. And yet how often did you say with Jacob, "How awesome is this shrine!"?

No other word but awesome describes what happened to you in that very ordinary church, for there you changed. It was as if God held that holy house in suspended animation in order that he might work on you. Outside in the streets all else was movement; the world turned so fast that in contrast you stood still. Outside you were always the same while the world was different each morning. In that quiet nave, however, you became a new world turning, whirling on your axis, speeding in your orbit while the universe around you, the stars and planets of this church, slowed and stopped. Only the red and blue and green moved, advancing across the floor, firing you with longing, aspiration, love, regret, joy, resurrection. As your heart passed in and out of the meteor shower cascading through the stained glass, it was energized; you became God's armature. How awesome was this shrine.

33

Now, all of Jacob's stairway was bathed in color; your very soul mounted in ascending spirals to the golden door beneath the blood red lamp. And written there upon the gate, Bethel, the house of God, Jacob's name for the shrine at the foot of the ladder. Here is the reason this simple chapel has always meant so much to you: You came to see it not as a magic castle where quick and easy answers would make life a dream, but as a path to God, a place in which to be convinced of his presence. In this holy house, you would pass through that current of divine love beaming from the west windows; that love was life to you, motive and means for growth in and toward the Lord. There God held all else still while you turned and leapt and danced and flew in and through and around and up that dazzling spectrum, that avenue of colors, that way of light to truth.

Old Mrs. Cracking Knees is probably gone by now. And pastors will catch the remodeling bug. But in your memory the old church remains the same; the feeling of the place will never fade, those sights and sounds that once emboldened you to ask for nothing short of divine power. For that, you know, is what each of us seeks that we may right the world's wrongs and bring good out of evil. It is the treasure of Bethel, the powerhouse of God.

Before the tabernacle in the circle of light cast by the constant flame, believers kneel in wonder, knowing that behind the golden doors lies the focus of God's urgent mercy upon humankind. The love that created and now animates the universe is concentrated in the grain of the harvest, once ground to dust then reformed and miraculously transformed to become the dynamic catalyst of everlasting life. The transforming power of love draws the broken of the earth to the hope of being made whole, to the prospect of entering that world veiled in watered silk and experiencing divine revitalization.

34

The allure of prayer before the tabernacle can be summed up in one word: dynamism. Not only does the praying person enter the holy house of God, that sacred space called church, but, in drawing near the new Ark of the Covenant, he or she submits to the movement of divine love that finds its locus of greatest intensity in the Real Presence of Jesus Christ. Through Christ, the Father continually re-creates the world in his own image; this re-formation is love's project, and love that emanates from the Godhead is never static. Divine love by its nature is the source of humankind's renewal. So, to approach the tabernacle is to open one's innermost being to the naked force of God's power to change and purify the human spirit. All authentic prayers in the charged circle cast by the tabernacle lamp are different ways of saying, "I am willing to be caught up." The words may be those of petition, thanksgiving, or adoration, but the act of the soul is one of weighing anchor, of launching the earth-bound self into the midst of the flashing orbits of God's loving purposes.

The attraction of this most intimate of meditations is rightly accompanied by a trace of holy fear. God's power is limitless and often surprising. As he builds his new world soul upon soul, he reaches first for those who reach for him.

Your wholehearted desire to open yourself to the Real Presence gives the Creator *carte blanche* to use your resolution, your good will, your vulnerability. He will take that which is pure and selfless in your heart and make it a part of the world's transfiguration. He will take that which is impure and selfish and reintegrate it for the renewal of your spirit. If you have cast off enough of what weighs most of us down, you may well be swept away by the music of divine recreation. You may find yourself shuttling between memories of what was and dreams of what could be, dreams just on the verge of realization, waiting only for you to shed a bit more self-concern. And, lest fear of the new stymie your approach to majesty, remember it is the compassionate Savior who leads you; he will not allow you to come to harm.

Find your place before those golden doors today. Bring with you only the simplest of words, the slightest of desires, the lightest of cares. Enter God's galaxy of love. Let what could be become what is. Let your spirit be swept away by the invisible movement of God's love for you and for his world. He waits there for you at the center, projecting through his Son, the model of reality, a vision of the new creation. He keeps a place for you. Find your place with him.

Stand with me, LORD, upon the threshold.
    Mind not my reluctance
        for it is a giant step and bold—
           this giving all, this letting go—
      to urge on one so self-controlled.
    Though the invitation is serenely offered,
        my heartbeat quickens;
           your hand is sure upon my shoulder
             yet I pause for fear
        of falling into love's uncharted sphere.

What is the price of losing
    my spirit to this vortex
of flashing grace and unsought transformation
        humming with Alleluias,
    hinting of hesitation?
Do I hear beneath a chorus of Hosannas
    a mother weeping,
    a confidant's denial,
        and from Gethsemane a voice
    seeming to demur?

If you, O LORD, my strength, my all,
    beheld the boundless glory
    beyond the gate
        and faltered,
    then who am I to rashly pass this way?

Guide of life, lead this timid soul.
    Beside you I shall quest
        beyond the point of no return,
            not to prove my courage
        nor to hear angelic choirs,
    but for the sweet certainty of your call.
        I will leave my footprint, LORD,
            on the golden sill, and rise or fall
                on eagles' wings with you,
        my strength, my all.
        Amen.

Free Wheeling

A Pharisee invited him to dine with him, and he entered the Pharisee's house and reclined at table. Now there was a sinful woman in the city who learned that he was at table in the house of the Pharisee. Bringing an alabaster flask of ointment, she stood behind him at his feet weeping and began to bathe his feet with her tears. Then she wiped them with her hair, kissed them, and anointed them with the ointment. When the Pharisee who had invited him saw this he said to himself, "If this man were a prophet, he would know who and what sort of woman this is who is touching him, that she is a sinner." Jesus said to him in reply, "Simon, I have something to say to you." "Tell me, teacher," he said. "Two people were in debt to a certain creditor; one owed five hundred days' wages and the other owed fifty. Since they were unable to repay the debt, he forgave it for both. Which of them will love him more?" Simon said in reply, "The one, I suppose, whose larger debt was forgiven." He said to him, "You have judged rightly." Then he turned to the woman and said to Simon, "Do you see this woman? When I entered your house, you did not give me water for my feet, but she has bathed them with her tears and wiped them with her hair. You did not give me a kiss, but she has not ceased kissing my feet since the time I entered. You did not anoint my head with oil, but she anointed my feet with ointment. So I tell you, her many sins have been forgiven; hence, she has shown great love" (Lk 7:36-47).

New, it wasn't. Nor dirt-free. Nor easy on the oil. But it was your first. The freakshow reflection from the glossy fender made you look ten feet tall. That's just how you felt. Mobile at last! "Free wheeling," it said in the ads. You were ready.

Sleep seemed never quite to bless you that first night when you lay in bed listening, guarding your maroon beauty from all the horrors a reckless world could visit upon a quiet street. How many times did you go to the window and admire that long, low hood, the chrome-splashed fender skirts, the one-piece rear window? Of course, you slept, but only until the faintest ray of light crept over the sill. The shade was up on purpose; not one moment of daylight would be wasted. In an act of sheer joy, you jumped out of bed and proclaimed your liberation by throwing your last three streetcar tokens into the Reynolds' back yard. Free wheeling, at last!

Our first automobiles have a mythic quality about them. Constantly charged by youthful yearning, our dreams of freedom almost always have a car in them. For many, that car is the constant centerpiece of fantasy. It occupies our daytime reveries, soothes when sleep eludes us at night. It is the bone of contention that sours relationships with those who hold our fate in their hands. That electric dream of motorized independence makes the youth who lately wouldn't cross the room to lift a dollar from the floor now grow pale from working for nickels. All in pursuit of the mythic steed that will carry him or her away, no matter where, as long as it's elsewhere.

The myth of the automobile is never realized. In dreams of speed and freedom, the car is always lower than practical, faster than possible, cheaper than feasible. That day when you rumbled off the used car lot was the day of the great compromise. You found you couldn't afford the sleek two-year-old that you had been admiring on its raised platform for weeks. You settled on one in the back row, a ground level car you hadn't seen, although the whorls of dust on the roof said it had been waiting for you for some time. The battery, though, hadn't been so patient; a jump start was necessary to shock the engine into a rough kind of life. The floor mats were threadbare. The right rearview mirror was cracked. Plenty of blue smoke, but just at first. By the time you made the circuit of the block, the salesman knew you were his. You could afford this one; the man at the bank frowned at your profligacy, but approved the loan. He thought of himself as a keen judge of character; the odds were better than fifty-fifty that your solvency would outlive the coming demythologization.

Now, endurance was required; for an unknown length of time you would have to survive the critical stares of your friends. This wasn't the baby you told them you were going to get. It wasn't even close, but it had its redeeming features. No, the rust under the left taillight wasn't a redeeming feature. Neither was the dangling bumper guard, nor the dented hubcap, nor the fading roof, broken horn ring, squeaking trunk lid or missing radio. There was only one redeeming feature—motion, that flight through the haze of authority to freedom. Thus, you weren't resentful that the bones had been numbered; your wheelless friends were simply satisfying themselves that they had brought you back down to their humble level of immobility. The obligatory ritual of criticism having exorcised the green-eyed devil, you and your comrades could now get down to the business of pretending the car was perfect and begin to enjoy together this miracle of motion and its magic ways. You could burn a bit of rubber at a stoplight. The tires would give a satisfying screech as you circled the drive-in. Girls would turn their heads and wave. After that first day, your pals mentioned the blemishes on your dream machine only when provoked by your braggadocio or when their need for transport was overcome by a particularly sharp stab of envy. Every once in a while, they reminded you that pretense was indeed a fragile flower in the hot garden of youth.

Pretense was not the favorite bloom in the garden of a good Pharisee, at least not someone else's pretense, and especially that fiction Jesus seems to encourage in the presence of sinful people. The host in Luke's gospel is not about to pretend to himself that the woman who anointed Jesus is anything but a notorious wanton. He exercises what he sees to be his pharisaical right and judges her; in the process, he also judges Jesus to be not a true prophet since a prophet would not knowingly allow a public sinner to touch him. Simon's assumption is that Jesus either pretends to be a prophet or, if he is genuine, pretends to be blind to the woman's sullied past.

Jesus does not pretend. He sees the woman's checkered reputation as clearly as you saw the rust and dents in your first car. They were more painfully obvious to you than to even the most critical of your companions. This blemished beauty was the fruit of your sweat and your saving. It was the embodiment of your ideal; you had invested your whole life in this machine. If it ran rough, you ran rough. If it soared, you soared. Jesus was the model for every human being. Each man and woman was created through him. The stains on this woman's soul were an insult to Jesus, the template of humankind. He could not pretend not to see her as she was, for he alone knew what she should be.

You did not pretend that there were no flaws in your car; it was impossible for you to overlook them. Rather, they receded in comparison to the freedom, prestige and power that car brought you. The virtues of your maroon beauty outweighed her vices. So also with "the woman in the town known to be a sinner" and Jesus. That he allowed her to touch him was not pretense but stark honesty. His willingness to receive her obeisance came from a heart that felt the good in her, a good that he could draw out and bring to flower. His acceptance of her act was a declaration of his confidence in her best intention. He did not pretend she was perfect; he did not overlook her sins any more than you were able to overlook the flaws in your car. You named them every time you stepped on the running board: dents, rattles, rust, wear. Jesus names them every time we allow our consciences to echo his words: envy, gluttony, sloth, pride, anger, avarice, lust. But you got in the car and drove; you could do no other, for this baby was your salvation. And Jesus gets into our world and lives with us. He can do no other, for he was sent to be our salvation.

Each of us comes to prayer hat in hand. It is not simply deference to our Creator that brings us to our knees; we bow our heads under the weight of imperfection. The heightened sensitivity that must accompany prayerful discernment also makes us acutely aware of the misuse of the very faculties that enable us to pray. These hands folded so piously were engaged in twisting God's plan just hours ago. This tongue bold enough to pronounce the name of the Savior lately shattered a neighbor's self-respect. The mind and heart we struggle to lift up now still bear traces of bitter envy and wisps of dreams of sweet revenge.

Yet despite the baggage of brokenness, we go on praying. Like refugees at the emigration counter, we put down our embarrassingly battered luggage and wait for the opportunity to buy a ticket to a new life, a rearrangement of priorities, a reintegration of things as they are. While on the surface our petitions describe our ideas of escape from pain or want or fear, the real but often unperceived prize of prayer is some kind of reconciliation of our imperfections. Because we are afraid of the rigors supposedly imposed upon the quest for perfection, we pray not to be made perfect but to accept, and to be accepted with, our imperfections, to be issued a ticket and a baggage check.

Part of any prayer must be at least the implied expression of our claim on God to accept us as we are. We base this claim on the words and deeds of God's acceptance-made-flesh. Jesus' parables, such as that of the Pharisee and the tax collector, make us bold enough to expect, at the minimum, divine tolerance. "But the tax collector stood off at a distance and would not even raise his eyes to heaven but beat his breast and prayed, 'O God, be merciful to me a sinner'"' (Lk 18:13). He was justified, that is, reconciled, while the Pharisee was merely perfect. Prayer leads us beyond striving for some elusive perfection to the freedom of reconciliation.

Reconciliation is another way of describing liberation from earthly comparisons. Those envious friends, who made sure you knew that first car didn't measure up, based their expectations on what the tastemakers deemed acceptable: not a spot of rust, no frayed upholstery, but flashing speed, limitless power, obvious prestige. Judgment had been passed and you were sentenced to another term of embarrassment. Authentic prayer includes the acknowledgment that the only Judge who counts bends down to reform and renew those things in us which are patently unwholesome and dismiss our fears about not measuring up to the world's standards. When God, through Christ, reconciled us to himself, he made us free men and women, citizens of a new creation (see 2 Cor 5:11-21). Thus, we pray in freedom, setting aside the burden of sin and the threat of judgment. Like the tax collector, we cannot forget what we have done, yet we are certain enough of God's mercy to ask him to overlook our failures. As for worldly opinion, the very act of going to prayer proclaims our independence from what is transitory. Good prayer is timeless. We rest secure in prayer, confident that God is healing that which is broken in us, transforming our weaknesses into strengths, all the while loving every part of us as we accept his acceptance.

Free Wheeling

O God,
I give you thanks
  that I am not like him
  sniveling there in the back row,
  bending beneath the weight of his woe.
I come to you with clean hands
  and a perfect record
  of fasting and giving
  and righteous living.
Examine my spiritual progress;
  find nothing amiss,
  an open book eager for your perusal,
  ready and waiting for your approval.
Probe my thoughts,
  the essence of my being,
  my motives, intentions,
  my honorable mentions.

  Mighty Father,
do you turn away
  from the radiance of my repute?
  Surely Omnipotence can reply
  to another sun in the sky.
Look not upon that figure in the shadows,
  those rounded shoulders
  shaking in self-accusation,
  meant to elicit consolation.
He is not one of us, LORD,
  not a star serenely set in heaven
  but a victim of dereliction
  fallen on the path to perfection.
Rather, see me in my splendor:
  let your majesty be mirrored,
  wisdom, power full returned,
  in the holiness I've earned.

O Judge most just,
your attention to the front seat, please,
    to your servant so obedient,
    to the jots and tittles in my purse,
    to the list of prayers that I rehearse.
Pay no heed to sighs behind us,
    the gasp of guilt escaping
    lips pressed upon the back of the pew
    ratcheting out Psalm Twenty-Two.
Against the blinding coalescence of our light,
    you can barely see the red-stained palms
    or the threadbare purple robe
    of one more bleakly faithful Job.
Not our kind at all, LORD;
    still, I will forgive your obvious distraction
    and join you in majestically expressing
    our deep concern in brief but heartfelt blessing:
    Amen.

Thieves Like Us

But now in Christ Jesus you who once were far off have become near by the blood of Christ.

For he is our peace, he who made both one and broke down the dividing wall of enmity, through his flesh, abolishing the law with its commandments and legal claims, that he might create in himself one new person in place of the two, thus establishing peace, and might reconcile both with God, in one body, through the cross, putting that enmity to death by it. He came and preached peace to you who were far off and peace to those who were near, for through him we both have access in one Spirit to the Father.

So then you are no longer strangers and sojourners, but you are fellow citizens with the holy ones and members of the household of God (Eph 2:13-19).

The vacant block had filled up slowly. Long, dark cars and half-ton trucks, all mud-splashed from a night on the road, gasped and fell silent. Alien license plates crawled by: Fla., Tex., Miss., W. Va., Okla. Strange people emerged from their vehicles. Lanky men unfolding themselves from the bowels of pre-war Cadillacs and Lincolns. Women smoking to-beat-the-band. Scrawny kids began working without supervision, laying the necessary groundwork for raising the small tents and assembling the rides. In the middle of the square, on the brass poles of the floorless merry-go-round, gaudy horses were hung, suspended over nothing, unanchored, swaying in the wind like a wild pack in a corral waiting to bust the fence when your back is turned. At the end of what would be the midway, the ferris wheel took on fragile seats that swung back and forth, wagging heads taunting the coward. All the big rides sneered at the fainthearted, "Are you brave enough to be hurled straight into the sky? Have you the courage to face the hard truth that, while you are tilting and whirling and spinning, one tiny bolt may snap and . . . ?"

Flanking the ominous rides were two long rows of booths, each of which offered something for nothing. A nickel or a dime was nothing; the chance to win a genuine space helmet or an expensive doll was quite something. And, so easy: pull a tab, jerk a string, fire a rifle, pitch a baseball, spin a wheel, break a balloon. What could be simpler!

The square was completed with the shows: freaks on one end, girls on the other. Bright stands for the barkers were already in place. Yvonne's ruffled swing was being attached to the top of her window. The dog-faced boy was washing his wife's hair.

In the midst of this measured industry stood the townsfolk, little knots of men who had for one day relinquished their benches in front of the bank, gaggles of housewives just passing by on the way home from the grocery store. No children yet; school let out at 3:15. Not wanting to appear interested, the elders would be gone by then. But interested they were, intensely curious about these people of the road and their strange looks. They stood in their groups with folded arms and pointed with their smug voices at "the look of that one" and "that's not the way I'd build a booth." Every year the good citizens would spend set-up day trying to figure out who these others were while intimating that it didn't make a hill of beans. Yvonne and the dogfaced boy and his wife and the tent men and the concessionaires and the operators were used to it. They got the same stares in every town, but never stared back. They just went about their business setting up, but sometimes a little after midnight when the lot had emptied, they laughed.

First Night was always half-price for children, little children who had to be accompanied by adults, of course. A double play, the carnies called it: Get the kiddies thirsty for another full-price night; get the parents who wouldn't be caught dead there to open their wallets. Aware of the trap, parents would make sure that they took home more than their share of prizes and sensations. In this way, every square in every town became a battlefield pitting the insiders against the outsiders with both the townies and the carnies assuming the role of the innocent party, the godly who must pull together to outsmart the barbarians.

Only the children would be immune to the palpable hostility which their elders would bring to this square tonight. Despite sharp parental warnings about "that kind of child," young nomads and potential burghers would mingle shyly at first, then run together behind the trailers or across the street to a back porch, and end by sharing their treasures: an arrowhead, a mammy doll, a horned toad, a seashell necklace. The kids didn't know any better. They would have to grow a little more, stumble into their teens before they could call their parents' prejudices their own. It was too early to fear the outsider if you weren't old enough to appreciate the stories: The little girl who was carried away when the carnival left town. The boy who was kept in jail causing his parents to abandon the season. And for what reason, what was the mistake, what was the crime? The only reason ever given for these fanciful outrages was "the difference." In appearance, in speech, in background, in religion, in morality, they were different from us; that's why they did those things. The kids, though, couldn't understand these big words, couldn't grasp the magnitude of the danger; they only saw other kids.

You and I have learned a lot of big words since the carnival came to town. We know what enmity means, and hostility, and prejudice. Most of us didn't have to go to the dictionary to learn these words; they seemed to spring fully defined from the action of a stranger. We learned by experience and by example that outsiders cannot be trusted, that strangers ridicule our customs, that those who are different threaten the tightly-knit communities in which we've invested our hopes. We are the Jews and Gentiles of the letter to the Ephesians, separated by the barrier called stereotype, prevented from perceiving the true character of the other because of the actions of one or two of his brothers or sisters.

49

Paul tells us that in Christ the barrier of stereotype has been broken down. Not only does the blood of Christ cleanse our vision so that we can perceive hearts, it has washed away the contradictory laws by which we and they once lived. In his death and resurrection, a new covenant was born, a reconciliation that has re-created us, formed us into a new family. In making us new men and new women, Christ has made us little children again; he has freed us to play with the others as brothers and sisters. The "good news of peace" calls us into the same household. Enmity gives way to childlike trust. The good news of the resurrection of Jesus is an invitation to enter a new union with God and with each other, one that will endure, for it withstood the ultimate dissolution. The body of Christ lives on and we make up that body. We—nomads or homebodies, carnies or townies, sinners or saints—arm ourselves no longer against the alien; rather, with the wide-eyed innocence and trusting acceptance of a child at the carnival, we seek in each new face the lineage of our common Father.

The most difficult prayer of all is the petition to be made more vulnerable. Often, injury brings us to prayer in the first place. A slight, a snub by friend or foe confirms our belief that our hearts are too tender for the push and shove of this world. So we turn to Christ, the wounded-healer, for consolation. He graciously pours out his balm of love upon our chafed souls, then goes a step farther. Even as our optimism is restored by the Divine Physician, we are being strengthened for a jarring reintroduction to a ministry that has proven most unwelcome in the past, namely, turning the other cheek.

If the world is to be made up of "strangers and sojourners no longer," then Christians have to risk rejection in extending the hand of fellowship to those who stand apart. The operative prayer in this ministry of reconciliation is a plea that hearts of

50

stone may become hearts of flesh. Because he or she wants so much to accept, and to know the profound acceptance of, another, the praying person calls out for nothing less than the courage to be wounded more deeply. This is the essence of self-sacrifice, the motive of each of Christ's words and deeds, the polestar of reconciliation. Yet, in the silence of solitary prayer, with the self-image still smarting from a rebuff, common sense whispers, "Don't be a glutton for punishment."

Reconciliation requires not gluttony but a certain spiritual discipline, not a masochistic thirst for rejection, but an inner wisdom of acceptance and endurance based on Jesus' call to turn the other cheek. His reversal of the old law of vengeance is more than moral revaluation; offering no resistance to injury is the first practical step in evangelization, an earnest payment which may have to be offered again and again (see Mt 5:38-42). In bringing two disparate groups or individual antagonists together, movement awaits the consistently advanced proof that neither party has anything to fear. That surety will probably require a series of tests. At least one of the parties must accept the probing lance no matter how deep or frequent the thrust. The ability to offer that kind of acceptance is the object of the prayer for vulnerability.

In your prayer, by all means seek any necessary consolation. The dagger of enmity cuts no less deeply for being undeserved. God sends his Son to touch your unjustly injured heart with his healing hand and to assure you that you didn't make a mistake in praying for stone to become flesh. But do not forget that prayer is also for your continued openness to those beyond the pale, the strangers and aliens who came to town expecting a fight. For their sakes, you pray for strength, not for an outer shell of armor which will deflect even the most innocuous barbs, but for the interior endurance to absorb the thrusts born of envy and fear that may well foretell a reciprocal openness across the barricades. Pray to retain your heart of flesh, a heart that accepts, a heart that conquers through love and humility.

Remember me, Jesus?
    The woman at the well,
    the half-caste with the forbidden cup
    and the unpleasant past.
    You drank
        and promised me living water.
    Now, I am thirsty.

Remember me, Jesus?
    The mother of Canaan
    begging like a dog under the table
    for a scrap of compassion.
    You spoke
        and freed my child.
    Now, I am possessed.

Remember me, Jesus?
    The centurion from Rome
    amazed at your absolute authority
    over my servant's malady.
    You commanded
        and the boy was cured.
    Now, I will serve you.

Remember me, Jesus?
    One of the billion supplicants
    separated by two thousand years and miles,
    yearning for communion.
    You asked
        that I be your disciple.
    Now, I will follow you.
        Amen.

Picnic

Then the wolf shall be a guest of the lamb.
    and the leopard shall lie down with the kid;
The calf and the young lion shall browse together,
    with a little child to guide them.
The cow and the bear shall be neighbors,
    together their young shall rest;
    the lion shall eat hay like the ox.
The baby shall play by the cobra's den,
    and the child lay his hand on the adder's lair.
There shall be no harm or ruin on all my holy
    mountain;
      for the earth shall be filled
        with knowledge of the LORD,
      as water covers the sea (Is 11:6-9).

    The boys always measured your picnics by what wasn't there. They assigned a letter value to the importance of the items left waiting back in the kitchen. A picnic at which nothing was forgotten was given an *A*. There had never been an *A* picnic. Butter or salt missing received a *B*. No catsup or mustard, a *C*. No soft drinks, a *D*. The *F* rating under which the most disastrous of your outings had completely collapsed was given for the absence of a can opener. On that memorable occasion, the thin screwdriver in the glove compartment proved too fragile an instrument to free the beans, the sardines, and the vienna sausages from their silvery vaults. To the utter joy of the dog, the rather large rock that finally did the job simultaneously distributed the food. That picnic was called on account of beans. Recriminations flew furiously in the car on the way home; to stop the bitter accusations of duty undone, you took the blame with a self-serving sigh and wondered if there were enough noodles in the pantry for macaroni and cheese. This thought you kept to yourself for the mere mention of this most economical of dishes would draw howls of protest from your passengers. The *F* this picnic received was bestowed not only for forgetting the can opener but also for adding insult to injury—macaroni and cheese.

F picnics were not the rule; most were *C*s with a few *B*s. You didn't absolutely need butter to enjoy a hamburger, nor catsup or mustard. These thoughtful touches helped, but their absence didn't outweigh the refreshment of the ice cold stream or the smell of pine needles on the fire or the feel of the breeze in your hair. Just being away from the city was enough. The boys wouldn't catch anything in the stream; you knew that and you suspected that despite their apparent enthusiasm they did too. Throwing a worm into the swift water was simply something they couldn't do in town. It was like lighting a fire outside or smelling just plain air instead of engine fumes—that which was forbidden by the moil of circumstance 45 minutes from here was allowed in this Eden. The laws of metropolitan nature had been overturned: Bus horns gave way to birdsong, the neighboring row of houses disappeared in favor of a horizon, a million and a half people became six. Some hand, some power had changed the rules so that for once you could compete on equal terms with the madness of the world, compete and, for a few hours at least, win.

Things happened on these *B* and *C* picnics, and even on the *D* outings, that didn't happen at home. Take laughter. You were sure that the kids laughed at home, but it was hard to hear them do so. The radio drowned out the weak chuckle, or you missed it because you were really listening for the screams. At the picnic laughter lasted, went all the way from the chortle through the guffaw to the satisfied sigh of mirth. They didn't laugh like that in the city. Take discovery. At home, every hour echoed the last, every apartment had the same floor plan, every car was a Ford. On picnic day, the kids' fingers were stiff from pointing out things they had never seen before: a diving hawk, a petrified limb. They babbled on, using words of wonder you hadn't heard since they were in kindergarten. Take kindness. The ball game was conducted in a soft cloud of apologies and pardons for wild pitches and overenthusiastic tags. The hard-edged smirks of the city melted into sloppy smiles in the warm sun. In just 45 minutes, you had driven through a tunnel of trees to emerge in a different realm, a kingdom where people sat on the grass and hugged their knees for joy, a place where the atmosphere breathed into you, saving you the effort, filling your soul with a sense of crisp reality that the city could not provide. It was as if the very earth was "filled with knowledge of the Lord."

Why is it so difficult to know the Lord in the city? Is he not present there as intensely as he was on your idyllic outings? Of course, the Lord is everywhere the same, but we are not. Chameleon-like, we take on the color of the latest distraction. The city is a thousand things clamoring for our attention: pay this, buy that, heed the warning, cross, don't cross, pay fare here, slow down, speed up, parking prohibited. That's the trouble with city life; parking is usually prohibited. You know the Lord is present; his reality fairly overpowers you at times. Still, you cannot stop to acknowledge him because parking is prohibited. The next mile, the next block, the next yard must be covered with alacrity, for to fall behind is to feel the hot breath of the wolf. The city is not filled with the knowledge of the Lord; the wolf will join the lamb for dinner in town only if the lamb is the entree.

In the realm of the spirit, city life can grip the heart of the farmer as easily as it squeezes the soul of the harried commuter. No one is immune from the distractions that prohibit the prayerful pause. You don't have to live in a bustling metropolis to grow spiritually dull; the daily agenda of the monk in his solitude can be just as swollen with secular concerns.

The remedy for a schedule lacking room for God is not physical flight from your surroundings; rather, it is the deliberate choice to come away with the Lord, away from the city life that prohibits knowledge of him. This prayerful pause must be prepared for as earnestly as you made ready for those picnics of the past. First, you must decide to pray. Then, you determine the best time of day to pray and resolve to be faithful to that time. Next, find a place to pray, a room congenial to silent meditation. Posture is important as well as the kinds of prayer that suit you and their arrangement. Finally, you must decide to listen, for half or more of prayer is listening. From time to time you will omit a step in your preparation; this is as inevitable as the missing catsup at the picnic. Continue to pray anyway. God does not grade your prayer. In fact, he may be using your forgetfulness to teach you something new about prayer. God always brings the can opener.

The city-soul gives up on prayer too easily. Because he or she has experienced profound communion with God so rarely, because meaningful meditation is remembered as the consequence of a perfect intersection of time, place and solitude, many an otherwise prudent Christian writes off rather hastily the possibility of engaging in fruitful prayer amid the tensions and hubbub of everyday life. The idea of praying with others— family members, no less—in a house alive with distractions is almost an insult to the fond memory of that day on the mountain trail when God's voice was in the wind.

The truth is that we do not live by peak experiences. Yes, we are inspired by the extraordinary insight or emotion; new directions, renewed hopes flow from the vacation or retreat, but we are sustained in the everyday by what happens each day. The praying person lives in a world of routine and must make prayer part of that routine. Abiding spiritual sustenance requires a certain arrangement of the immediate environment. The theme of the prayer may stretch back to an experience of Eden, but the words, feelings and petitions are molded by current events, and current events, those that make a daily difference in our lives, happen at home. The fortunate who can pray each day in a hushed basilica are thrice blest; the rest of us must build temporary chapels in a transient world. Like the Hebrews of old, we pitch a tent each night and wait for the presence of the Lord to be revealed.

Because in most cases that tent must be stitched from scraps of stolen moments, it flaps with distraction. Now taut with time's constraints, now loose enough to permit the escape of other family members, it is a meeting place of harried hopes and split-second silences. There is really only one saving grace in praying at home. God wants us to. Simple logic forces the Christian to a conclusion that seems to contradict the nature of modern society:

We should want what God wants.

Home is the only place where we can do what we want.

God wants us to pray every day.

Ergo, we should attempt to pray at home.

Usually, it's no picnic. The whispering stream of treasured memory becomes a bubbling pot on the stove. Birdsong is squeezed into baby's cry. Silence is punctuated by the shriek of a siren. And at least one family member, somewhere close by in loud rebellion, is stubbornly against the whole enterprise. Still, we sit in a circle, sometimes a circle of one, and thumb the Bible, finger the rosary, sweat over spontaneous prayer because... because it happened to us once in a peaceable kingdom. The equivalent of a child with his hand on the adder's lair and a leopard lying down with the kid was soul-probing, heart-singing prayer. We spoke with God and he was not fearsome. We showed him the depths of our soul and he did not despise us. Our memory may retouch and embellish the picture, but the primary colors cannot be obscured. We prayed, really prayed, once, twice...

and we want to pray again. Back there then a secret was revealed; now it must be told. We want those who share our tent to know the warm, encouraging, compassionate, refreshing presence of God. Against all common sense, against the logic of striving and ambition, we clear a place and a time in a room papered with schedules so that our little world may be ''filled with knowledge of the Lord.''

Can you hear me, LORD,
above that banging on the wall,
that cumbrous, riddled wrecking ball
   seeking friend in flaw and fissure,
      muffling pure petition and response
      even in the crystal chambers
      of my heart?

Prayer is so easy on paper:
words black on white from a pen
softly scratching in a cloister.
   See the tonsured head,
      the silent lips forming Aves and Paters
      above the rounded sounds, perfect spheres
      of adoration.

You can hear him, LORD,
praising without words the Word
spoken in silence,
   while I shout my soul out
      stretching my voice to pierce the din
      and wonder deep within if anyone
      is listening.

Could it be your arm, Lord,
which swings that blue-green globe
against these brittle ramparts?
    As once you razed the monkish cell
        to free a friar's fervent pleas,
        do you now hurl the world
        at my utopia?

A prayer to you, Lord:
From tumbled suppositions,
upon the swerving earth I leap—
    suddenly unsure of form or invocation—
        to offer ragged rings of supplication
        in chorus with the stuttering
        who only know their need.
        Amen.

Steam Heat

Jesus said: "I have come to set the earth on fire, and how I wish it were already blazing! There is a baptism with which I must be baptized, and how great is my anguish until it is accomplished! Do you think that I have come to establish peace on the earth? No, I tell you, but rather division" (Lk 12:49-51).

A startling sound, sharp and isolated like a marble dropped on a glass table top and caught on the bounce, a bubble of steam bursting in a rusting pipe deep within the bowels of the building. This single sound, echoless, shorn of lineage, seemingly unable to beget another, was nevertheless the initial crack in the bell jar of silence. You would lie still and cold, straining to hear the next bubble explode. It had to be perceptibly louder to herald the heat. If there was not another hollow report, it meant the super had merely dropped a wrench on a pipe. If there was a second sound, but softer, weaker, the cause could be simple contraction of metal in the cold. Only progressively stronger signals and a steady increase in their frequency would convince you that a flame indeed caressed the frozen belly of the boiler, tickled it with fiery fingers until the boisterous laugh rose to your radiator and set it to bouncing in furious mirth.

Those popping, dancing, singing radiators meant the apartment would soon be pliant again. Chairs stiffly hugging themselves would now open to receive you in warm embrace. Rigid bedsheets would grow limp in gratitude. The polar air that pinched your nostrils would swing 180 degrees, opening your pores to the humid kiss of a tropical rain forest. So what if this mid-winter thaw was accompanied by jungle drums and pulsing rhythms? What matter if the sizzling radiator barely constrained a hurricane of shrieks and moans? You and those you loved and everyone in every flat in this dyspeptic building were on the verge of being *warm*.

They came in all shapes and sizes, these bellicose buddhas that radiated heat so fiercely when under pressure that you had to stand back, fearful that, like the face of Moses, yours would glow from concourse with the deity. There were dainty, pressed-steel radiators in posh apartments. There were slim-vaned, smooth-sided art deco models that added to the ambience of efficiency in downtown offices. Then there were the Big Berthas, cast iron behemoths that stood in the corners of drafty bedrooms and dared you to get close, taunted you with warmth while spitting steam at you from the safety valve. Many years before at the foundry, an elfin spirit had carved into the mold apples and pears in bas relief, delicate sunbursts, tiny acorns. In your bedroom after 20 coats of paint, these fragile sculptures had receded, seemingly drawn into the molten iron. You wondered now and then if under all the paint, the slim tracery glowed red like rivulets of lava as the iron sizzled and sighed.

For all the thrashing and throbbing that signaled the arrival of hot water at your floor, the final act was carried out with quiet dignity. Once the super had made his always premature decision favoring economy over comfort, things settled down rapidly. The pleasant gurgle of moving water was a lullaby compared to the earlier noise of battle. A pop and a bump here and there and it was all over in a matter of minutes. The flats quieted floor by floor. The chilly air crept around you silently like a coward compared to the brassy embrace of the heat. When would you hear that rollicking tune again? Soon, you hoped, for the night was cold.

When we let zeal for the Christian way bubble up in our lives, an ardent flow of good intentions encircles our hearts, warming our hands, setting our feet to moving with the Lord of the dance. We rejoice to know again the confidence of single-minded witness. Nothing can deter us as we brashly challenge the world, knocking left and right those icy-fingered reserva-

62

tions that clutch at the coattails of our soul. We forge ahead into the cold wind; the heat of our commitment will draw all who shiver from hopelessness to our side. What good we shall do!

Then, reality sets in. We see the frozen landscape for what it is, a formidable obstacle course of contending interests. We begin to economize, to husband our resources. A full head of steam is not necessary to maintain a reasonable comfort level. Dancing and singing in the throes of Christian zeal spend too quickly the meager reserve of grace which God has given us. Besides, no one out there seems to be freezing, no one is rushing up with hands outspread to share our warmth. Why waste the fuel? Why spend the energy?

When the steam goes out of our Christian witness, it is not only you and I who feel the chill. As our commitment to mission grows cold, we cease radiating the love of God; those we live among stiffen in disappointment, protecting themselves against the winter of the next promise unkept. "So fervent was he," they say, "so bubbling was she with confidence in God's presence and protection. Now, the fire has died. We shall not make again the mistake of coming here for warmth."

With Christ we yearned to light a fire on the earth, but when we saw the consequences of the baptism he chose to receive and its implications for our settled and serene life, we thought better of allowing zeal its head. A little fervor goes a long way.

Even the most sanguine soul approaches with caution the prayer offered in spite of one's better judgment; for instance, the petition that zeal might overcome spiritual inertia. The best of Christians will try almost anything else first. Think of a particularly troublesome situation in your life. Most likely, pain is seeping from a botched relationship. Self-preservation is immediately operative. How can this feeling of unease be overcome?

First, the easy prayer for the easy answer: "Father in heaven, make my fickle friend a better person. Soften her heart. Give him a dose of divine compassion. If that fails, Lord of the quick fix, remove the fly from my ointment. Adjust the sun, moon and stars so that I will no longer have to deal with such an impossible person." Fortunately, God is not a personnel manager; he is not about to reconstruct the world to satisfy one person's devotion to expedience.

You are left with Plan B, the prayer that calls for a change in the petitioner. Prayer for zeal assumes that the status quo is unacceptable, that you are part of the status quo, and that you must take the first step in the healing process. This is the prayer of Jesus that the blaze be ignited on the earth only after it springs up in himself, the prayer that he might plunge into the baptism of suffering that was to be the first step in his father's plan of reconciliation. This zeal is a holy impatience for an improvement in things as they are, a bubbling up of courage from the wellsprings of Christian mission. Every praying person knows the self-protective hesitation that muffles this petition, the hundred arguments against the solitary commitment to reopen communication. As the old iron radiators rumbled ominously and finally spit steam, so will the comfortable soul protest the warming to a reformed relationship. It seems counterproductive to pray that your desires might give way to the needs of another. Thus, the necessity of a plea for the unleashing of zeal, that power deep within that overcomes an attachment to injured feelings. Only God can give this gift, for it is a manifestation of the love that he implants in even the most complacent heart.

The courage to invest the self in an attempt at renewal underlies any prayer for zeal. This courage, however, must be accompanied by a wisely restraining strength born not out of fear of change, but from the realization that zeal can get out of hand. The Christian who seeks to transform the status quo must be strong enough to marshal the forces within and to check the all-too-human tendency to explode a reasoned approach to change through holy impatience. There is something in each of us that would scorch the earth rather than pull the weeds. Though it finds a voice only infrequently in the New Testament, we can suppose that Jesus dealt with this temptation often. His commitment to the kingdom, while single-minded and urgent, had to be measured and deliberate lest the weakest of his followers be overwhelmed. You and I must handle the zeal for which we pray in the same way. Any healing process requires the blaze of ardor, but the result should be warmth rather than a firestorm. When he drove the money changers out of the Temple, Jesus was certainly consumed by zeal for his Father's house (see Jn 2:17). The careful reader will note, however, that he didn't burn the place down.

You have not asked me, LORD,
    to purify society
    or bridge the world of rich and poor.
My mandate, rather, speaks
    of everyday discipleship,
    a life poured out in drops of hope
upon the furrowed brows
    of neighbors, friends and foes alike,
    whose need is known to you alone.

Baptize the world, you said,
    and newly-missioned fishermen
    emboldened by your radiance,
made ardent by the sight
    of hope arisen from the dead,
    transcended ancient boundaries
to wake the sleeping earth
    as servants of the God-made-man
    whom they had seen and touched and heard.

I have not seen you, LORD,
    or shared with Peter, James, and John
    the glories in the Upper Room.
So even an attempt
    at humble witness to your Light
    requires the miracle of zeal.
Enkindle in my soul
    a flame of love for wanderers
    who search this little world of mine.
        Amen.

Kyrie, Eleison

Now that very day two of them were going to a village
seven miles from Jerusalem called Emmaus, and they
were conversing about all the things that had occurred.
And it happened that while they were conversing and
debating, Jesus himself drew near and walked with
them, but their eyes were prevented from recognizing
him. . . . As they approached the village to which they
were going, he gave the impression that he was going
on farther. But they urged him, "Stay with us, for it is
nearly evening and the day is almost over." So he went
in to stay with them. And it happened that, while he
was with them at table, he took bread, said the blessing,
broke it, and gave it to them. With that their eyes were
opened and they recognized him, but he vanished from
their sight. Then they said to each other, "Were not
our hearts burning [within us] while he spoke to us on
the way and opened the scriptures to us?" So they set
out at once and returned to Jerusalem where they
found gathered together the eleven and those with
them who were saying, "The LORD has truly been
raised and has appeared to Simon!" Then the two re-
counted what had taken place on the way and how he
was made known to them in the breaking of the bread
(Lk 24:13-16, 28-35).

Introibo ad altare Dei.
Ad Deum qui laetificat juventutem meam.
He hesitates there on the first step as if afraid to enter the
holy place. The two little boys in black and white mumble on,
lulling themselves back to dreamland after this early morning's
rude awakening. He stands between them in his stiff, square

chasuble, a reproachful ramrod to the oblivious Knecht brothers now slumping toward the arms of Morpheus.

Introibo.... Will he now finally go up? No, there is something that must be done, a cleansing, a perfective confession of all which holds him back from that unsullied table. *Confiteor Deo omnipotenti....*

Ostende nobis, Domine, misericordiam tuam.

Et salutare tuum da nobis

Mercy is given. He mounts three steps. Your yawn is a sigh of relief that, as always, you and the other sleepy supplicants are not permitted to enter the unseen gate that opened for him. Heavy eyes follow his progress, eyes lost in the deep green of the watered silk, eyes glistening in the candle glow reflected from the golden fleurs-de-lis and filigrees. Do not lose sight of him in the shadows, for he is your son at sacrifice. Each attendant at this altar offers this first-born as appeasement; this is the innocent lamb in whom you shall placate God.

Munda cor meum.... A scalding stream of grace pours forth from the holy book; it cascades down the steps and washes against the wounded hearts of those who stand in solitude. Now it stings your soul, a bath of fire cauterizing the flayed innocence that awakened you in the darkness last night. You take a body blow, inwardly reeling at the Gospel's indictment, not at all encouraged by the words of Christ but at least grateful that you can still hear them. Despite your sins, God has not inflicted upon you a mortal wound. *Laus tibi, Christe.*

Suscipe, sancte Pater, omnipotens aeterne Deus, hanc immaculatam hostiam....

Immaculatam? Superficially cleansed, perhaps, but painfully aware of the subterranean pools of concupiscence which lap against the sides of your soul, you notice the slight inclination of his head, the silent sign of offering. This is but rehearsal for that moment of dread when the truly immaculate host, the Christ of God, will slowly be revealed above the tonsured head. He will have beseeched the Almighty Father to transform this host of doubt and neglect into the spotless fleece of the Lamb of God. You shudder at the thought of the agony that the forces of nature must undergo to accommodate the words of consecration. Will that part of nature which you ruefully claim as your own endure it? *In spiritu humilitatis....*

> *Hanc igitur oblationem servitutis nostrae, sed et cunctae familiae tuae, quaesumus, Domine, ut placatus accipias....*

That which was foreshadowed is about to take place. As the tiny bell echoes in your mind, it becomes a warning gong, tolling the accusations of the Lamb soon to be born. In his hands the peace offering, so thin and fragile, will be transubstantiated into a brilliant circle of perfection held high to shame the segmented and sectored who bow in timid anticipation. They will survive the comparison, for they will not raise their eyes to meet it. You, too proud to bow, know you will not survive the sunburst of truth. *Hoc est enim corpus....* No, you will not genuflect as you step from the pew and rush into the street.

How thin was our concept of the Mass when we worshipped at the back of the priest. While many may feel a twinge of nostalgia for the roll of a Latin phrase, few of us would trade today's experience of Eucharistic community for an appearance before the Grand Inquisitor. With the disciples on the way to Emmaus, we are gratified to leave behind judgment of our cowardly ways in favor of a humble meal presided over by the One whose life we thought our sins had ended. The Emmaus meal, which we celebrate each Sunday, is living proof that our sins are not stronger than God's love, that we have been judged worthy of the most extraordinary acts by which God salvages our shipwrecked souls.

In concentrating our attention on our failures, the old Mass became a judicial proceeding in which the verdict had already been written. There was seldom an acquittal; the most one could hope for was a suspended sentence with probation. Probation allowed us to receive Communion while promoting the fiction that we were being perfected. To be sure, that liturgy was capable of sustaining moments of high drama; we loved the Pontifical Masses because the singing and the incense and the pomp took our minds off the certain judgment. In the last analysis, however, in those solemn sung Masses, we were simply taking our cases to a higher court.

There is little pomp and less theater in your parish Mass today. Be grateful for that. Grandiose rituals require distance, room for the sweeping movement, and that distance falls between you and the altar, between you and your Savior. He was not distant from those he met on the road in Luke's gospel. The Son of God sat down at table with them, explained the scriptures to them, broke bread with them in Eucharistic union.

Is this not a pretty good description of what happens in your church each Sunday? Come close to that holy table with confidence. There Jesus waits with mercy mild to judge you worthy of his friendship.

It is sad but true that many Catholics approach the reformed liturgy with the same attitudes which brought them to the Tridentine Mass: a hidden heart full of rueful reservations and special intentions seeking a narrow encounter with God, right in the middle of a family celebrating its history and hopes. Not a few find it hard to forget the time when language and architecture forced them to kneel in awe outside the mystery rather than stand and become a part of it. In those days, we came to church like Marley's ghost, encumbered with so many mea culpas that we were unable even to raise our heads and look at the host in its fleeting witness to purity. It was only natural to concentrate on personal predicaments and everyday escapes. The impenetrable Latin, a Communion rail as bulwark, the rigid movements of the priest said: Keep your distance. So we prayed by ourselves. Sin-ridden and monolingual, we were unworthy of what was going on *up there*.

Then it happened. One day there were plugs in the floor where the Communion rail stood. The choir sung a hymn by Martin Luther. And the priest had a front as well as a back. We weren't sure we liked it, but we went along, at least on the outside. Inside, it was still me and the Judge.

If there is a place for "me and the Judge," an empty chapel or a silent sewing room will provide it. Come to Mass to pray out loud, to join with others in voicing your common concerns for the human family. Come to glory in the very act of assembling, to rejoice in the miracle of being called to be part of an event that takes place nowhere else on earth: your community celebrating community.

Accepting this invitation is not easy for those still burdened with inhibitions fostered, at the very least, implicitly by the liturgies of an earlier day. Are we not just as unworthy of approaching the altar now as we were in 1950? The answer is yes, but... Then, we thought that imperfection and failure made us displeasing to God. Now, in a more open, more comforting ritual, we begin to see that while God despises sin, he embraces the sinner as part of a struggling community. He wants us to offer ourselves completely to him, to dedicate for his use even that which is weak so that his power may be made manifest. This dedication, this handing over is seen and celebrated most strikingly in the Eucharistic gathering where my weakness is balanced by your strength and my failure becomes your challenge.

On the Emmaus road, two men with much to be ashamed of. In flight from a dream turned to dust, they sought approval from each other for their cowardice by recounting the horrors which would shake even the faith of Abraham. A stranger exuding a mysterious calm heard them out, then made them recline at a table set by patriarchs and prophets. They ate the bread of angels but remained men. Their eyes were opened to the Master who affirmed the worth of his sinful disciples by the simple act of giving nourishment. He would not throw food to dogs.

Each Sunday, the Emmaus road to the Eucharistic celebration is strewn with doubts and disillusion. On the table lies God's judgment upon his wayward sons and daughters, yet we enter without fear; for in the hands of the One who was pierced for our offenses awaits not selective condemnation but unleavened compassion for the broken of the earth. "As I have done for you, you should also do" (Jn 13:15). He chose our path and gave his all; we offer him what little we are and rejoice that he has accepted us as fellow pilgrims. Father Bernard Häring says it best: "We do not go to Communion in order to be rewarded for our virtue. Rather, we joyfully accept the divine invitation, since we are aware of the gracious, merciful and healing love of Jesus and yearn to love him in return" (Bernard Häring, *Heart of Jesus,* Liguori, Mo.: Liguori Publications, 1983, p. 102).

Wandering, LORD, I wonder
    at your willingness to walk
    with such a capricious companion
    as I who revel in the deepest rut
    and dub the ditch a royal road.

Wandering LORD, I wonder
    why you so often leave the straight and narrow
    to comb the hedgerows, calling out
    to me the glories of the Paschal feast
    awaiting all who find the way.

Wondering LORD, I wander
    not to test the patience of the Shepherd
    but only to escape the odious comparison
    with those who stride so righteously
    to the banquet of the elect.

Kyrie, Eleison

Wondering, LORD, I wander
    in the grip of vincible confusion,
    knowing all the while this simple prayer
    would bring you running to my side:
    Here, way over here, am I.
        Amen.

Good Evening,
Mr. First-Nighter

After six days Jesus took Peter, James, and John his brother, and led them up a high mountain by themselves. And he was transfigured before them; his face shone like the sun and his clothes became white as light. And behold, Moses and Elijah appeared to them, conversing with him. Then Peter said to Jesus in reply, "LORD, it is good that we are here! If you wish, I will make three tents here, one for you, one for Moses, and one for Elijah." While he was still speaking, behold a bright cloud cast a shadow over them, then from the cloud came a voice that said, "This is my beloved Son with whom I am well pleased; listen to him." When the disciples heard this, they fell prostrate and were very much afraid. But Jesus came and touched them, saying, "Rise, and do not be afraid." And when the disciples raised their eyes, they saw no one else but Jesus alone (Mt 17:1-8).

Grand Central Station, crossroads of a million private lives, gigantic stage . . . the Shadow knows . . . the story that asks the question: Can a girl from a small mining town in the West find happiness as the wife of a wealthy and titled Englishman . . . did you say my golf clubs were in the closet, Molly . . . now, we're back to Miss McConnell again . . . how are Jane and Irma, my two little barber poles, one with . . . dream along with me . . . thanks for the memories . . . I don't hold with furniture that talks.

But we did, Mr. Moody. For 30 years we kept one ear

cocked on an ungainly contraption that countless industrial de-
signers had tried to turn into an unobtrusive piece of furniture.
They never succeeded. The radio always stood out. It grabbed
our attention because that was its business. Even at rest with the
tubes cold and that little green eye closed, it was an Aladdin's
Lamp waiting only to be touched to pour forth a world of emo-
tions. Radio was all emotion. Even the "facts" on Information
Please were merely evanescent stimuli for our imaginations.
Which was higher, Kilimanjaro or Mont Blanc? Who remembers? But what flights of mind, what dreams were conjured by
Kilimanjaro brooding over the humid jungles; Mont Blanc,
solid onyx polished with a snowy chamois.

You listened to the radio on purpose then. It was not background noise to mute the sirens in the street. You sat in your
easy chair or at your desk or behind the steering wheel and paid
attention, for you were bent on being transported from the
present time and place. Radio gave you permission not to be
someone else, but to be yourself in a new dimension, to see what
could have been had the planets stood in a different order. If
your mother had been an heiress, your orchestra would be playing at the Rose Room. If your grandfather had moved to Cali-
fornia, you would be starring on the *Lux Radio Theater*. The radio
took all the disparate strands of fate and luck and circumstance
and wove them into a vivid tapestry of imagination. The central
figure in the tapestry was you . . . you trading wisecracks with
Benny, you in a steamy tryst with Gable, you with your Tommy
gun in Chicago, you peering at a strange cylindrical object half
buried in a New Jersey meadow. The radio wove the tapestry
around you; it spoke to no one else. Thus, so pointedly ad-
dressed, you had to pay attention.

Crackling and humming, it had its way with you. Once
you gave over control of your imagination, the irrational became common sense, the outrageous, commonplace. If you had
not sought miracles, you would not have turned the knob. De-
pending solely on your suspension of disbelief, radio programs

had their origins in tenements where people laughed all the time, ranches where cowboys sang all the time, small towns where people constantly spoke of their deepest hopes and dreams. You believed it all; there were places where those things happened; there had to be a Dr. Christian and a Ma Perkins and a Professor Kropotkin, kindly folks who wore their inmost thoughts on their sleeves and said just the perfect thing to heal a broken heart. Now and then, your attention wavered; back into focus came the living room or the darkened highway making you wonder which was real and which was absurd. A moment to pick from the matted horsehair the brilliant thread of fantasy, and once more you wrapped yourself in the tapestry of imagination.

That kind of radio is just about gone. All news or all noise, radio barely challenges the imagination. And television? It sees everything, rendering the imagination redundant. But there is an instrument in your home that invites you to become part of another scene in another time, one that can transport you to faraway places with strange sounding names. It is called the Bible. The Holy Book unfurls for you a tapestry of stories woven together by God and offered to you each time you open its pages. By making full use of the imagery of the Bible, you can stand with Moses on Sinai, dance with David before the Temple, ride with Judas Maccabeus on guerilla sorties, dine with Jesus at a Pharisee's house, and help the blinded Saul into Damascus. Sacred Scripture is a highly colored account of God's desire to save his fickle, feckless people. Each of us can find a thread to call our own in the warp and woof of salvation history.

Try making a meditation in the same way you used to listen to the radio. Allow the movement and emotion of the drama to draw you into a Bible story. As an example, step into the scene described in Matthew 17:1-8. See the high mountain and feel the wind trying to separate you from your companions. How did you get here? Did you hear the Master at the seashore and drop everything to follow him? Stand in for Peter and remember all Jesus has told you right up to the prediction that he must suffer and die. And you protested this prophecy. What a gaffe. The gentle man from Nazareth chastised you severely. How frightening to hear him call anyone a devil! That's what he called you. Now the Master gives in to the wind and stands apart; slowly his whole body is suffused with light until at the height of the revelation even his robe radiates glory. For some reason, you are not surprised. You always saw him as more than a cut above. But now you begin to shake in your sandals as two figures emerge from the electric atmosphere surrounding the radiant Master: the Lawgiver and the Prophet, the fathers of Torah and Tradition. Then, all reason bows in submission to the Voice with the divine affirmation. It is too much. Your legs give way as your mind gives up to dreams of the New Jerusalem with your emerald throne slightly below and to the right of the Master.

In radio days, the story went by so fast that you had time only to take the place of one character per show. As you allow the Holy Spirit to guide you through scripture imaging, weave the complete design by taking each part. Stand in for James, then for John. Even Jesus will give up his place as he receives the seal of sonship. Feel the love and gratitude that comes with hearing that cosmic affirmation. Take the places of Elijah and Moses; experience the culmination of your preaching and leadership. Want to go higher? As the Father in heaven, you see your plan working; your smile is your Son transfigured.

Here, a caution for the overly cautious. Do not let yourself be cowed by the eminence of the person whose role you take. As the radio gave you permission to don Lucky Lindy's flight suit or catch the falling scepter of Edward VIII, so scripture imaging invites you to assume the pomp and privilege of Pharoah and Solomon, the mission and message of Jeremiah and Isaiah, the omniscience of the Creator, or the healing power of the Messiah.

Be not a fly on the wall but a major player in the middle of the action so that you may feel, react, contemplate, move and be moved. Remember, too, that fastidious theological ruminations need not precede entering the drama of the Bible. You don't have to be conversant with the latest theories on the messianic secret in order to appreciate the courage of Jesus or the doubts of his followers. Common sense will lead you to the goal of any scripture imaging, namely, to come to a fruitful insight about how God's work was done on a particular day in the history of salvation, and how it is being done in your day. Granted, the greater your interest in biblical matters, the more easily you will move among the characters in the scene, but the willingness to get involved is of far more importance than familiarity with the minutiae of scholarship. The primary object of the exercise is that moment in the uncoiling of the imagination that elicits your "Ah, ha!" and a new perspective on God's love for you. The Bible is above all else a love story. Can you think of a better use for the gift of imagination than to make that love more real to you?

So, let sacred scripture be your spiritual radio offering delight and drama at your command. Step into the sandals of the holy men and women whose stories are told there as they lead you through trial to triumph. Tug now and then at a brilliant thread in God's tapestry and see in your mind's eye his plan revealed.

O Master, let me rest my bones
against that wind-struck terebinth
beyond the grasp of your stern gaze.
The haste in your ascendant step
has weakened my naive resolve
to conquer Tabor's rocky slope.

You know, my Jesus, I began
with hopes of glory from on high,
but now amid the raging storm
I must repose and steel my nerves
against the searching lightning bolts
unleashed to seal and ratify.

The clouded peak awaits not me,
a fisherman unused to heights.
The urgent thunder calls for you;
upon your head whirls heaven's dove.
Go up, go up and let me dream
of bursting nets and wave-lapped shores.

And yet I know there waits above
a higher truth, a saving word;
so lift me, Master, from my fears,
that having come this far with you,
I may forsake the valley's charm
and know the upland's awful grace.
    Amen.

All the World's a Stage

The LORD said:
Since this people draws near with words only
 and honors me with their lips alone,
 though their hearts are far from me,
And their reverence for me has become
 routine observance of the precepts of men,
Therefore I will again deal with the people
 in surprising and wondrous fashion:
The wisdom of its wise men shall perish
 and the understanding of its prudent men be hid.
Woe to those who would hide their plans
 too deep for the LORD!
Who work in the dark, saying,
 "Who sees us, or who knows us?"
Your perversity is as though the potter
 were taken to be the clay:
As though what is made should say of its maker,
 "He made me not!"
Or the vessel should say of the potter,
 "He does not understand" (Is 29:13-16).

At dusk, each front porch became the stage of a little theater. As an audience of one, you strolled down your very own
Schubert Alley sampling this comedy, that melodrama, encouraging by your hearty greeting the players in their idealized revelations of the lives that went on behind them. Under a fly-
specked spotlight, a pair of young lovers sat so still, so desper-
ately muting their singing hearts, that the swing didn't creak. At
the far end in the shadows near the fern, her mother with her
yarn: knit one, purl two, listen. Two houses up, the fat man with
his palm fan and pitcher of beer, thinking thin thoughts, each

exhalation producing a resigned sigh from the wicker chair. Then came two spinster sisters; each had finally pinched off her longing for a man's strong arms only to be assaulted on a warm evening by the sight of the fat man in his sleeveless undershirt. While they sat with their backs to him and talked of etiquette, they thought of him, heard the noises he made.

Front porch dialogue had a soothing monotony. The plumber always said, "How's tricks?" His wife, "Evenin', y'all." He was an Elk; she was from the South, but not that far south. The captain's wife, "Nice night," except when the sea brought the captain back and the porch was dark. Little girls invariably giggled at the oddity of your presence on a public sidewalk; little boys said, "Hi-yuh," like Gary Cooper. All these were theater sounds, meant to convey a bit more than was acutally there.

Porch players loved their theaters, first, because they were elevated. Sitting at least three feet off the ground produced a feeling of control. Like a bus driver, one could see well down the street. There were no surprises when sitting three feet off the ground. A person could predict things, tell what was coming long before people on the sidewalk even had a clue. And there was the balustrade that kept one safe from any outside intrusion. That half-wall was as thick as the brick it was made of, and as solid. The porch was impregnable to ruffian, peddler and night frights alike. But the best part of porch life had to be the opportunity it afforded the habitué to be someone else.

The sensitive stroller would note that none of the *personae* assumed by these players diverged radically from that lot chosen for them by the Almighty. The milkman didn't become a ringmaster when the porch light fell on him; he became a slightly rarefied milkman, a Provisioner of Rich Cream and Lightly Salted Butter. He left his low truck and mounted the five steps to the stage, there to speak, in the noble cadence of the Globe, of ghosts seen in the cemeteries of boyhood. He wanted to frighten the neighbor's kids just enough to make them take comfort with him and his childless wife. His route customers, however, told him he talked too fast when totting up their bills.

The chief teller at the bank let twining plants grow wild over his balustrade and called out greetings in a voice that slapped you on the back. His good will runneth over, splashed the unprepared with warm evening sunshine. Many on promenade forgot for a moment the hunched shoulders under the black eyeshade behind the high marble counter, but he never did.

The butcher's wife made of Early American not a period but a crusade. Everything was slip-covered in prints: the cushions on the swing and chairs, door panels, pillows for the flower pots, pillows for the feet, pillows for the cat. What wasn't cushioned in 13-starred flags and musketry was lathe-turned wood. The balustrade held 52 turned posts on either side of the screened door. Each of the three rocking chairs was made of exactly 37 pieces of turned wood. Slim, sculptured posts supported the occasional tables and held up the lamps and imprisoned the canary. A fastidious, homely, cradle-rocking hand had arranged all this. Yet, the butcher's wife was said to "run around" while he bowled in three leagues.

Every porch on this bourgeois Broadway starred actors and actresses who played primarily to the critics, to the blasé strollers whose disdainful glances could devastate the artiste. They weren't always honest about what went on backstage. Inside, in the houses where their souls dwelled, dissatisfaction soured the air. Reality was vinegar and someone had left the bottle open. Out on the porch, though, when evening furred the sharp outline of truth, a man could be stronger, a woman more alluring. Not that *anything* was possible in the glow of the porch light; just that something was possible, something different.

Today, a front porch is rarely a part of a new house. We don't have time for sitting and rocking. We don't want to brave the elements when just inside the door is the thermostat. But we still put on our sad vignettes, still sit before our make-up mirrors and apply vain conceits. Now the workplace becomes our theater. While resenting the boss' imperial style, we flatter her, play the toady, distort our consciences to the point of physical pain, so that she might look favorably on the character we portray. Now our friendships dictate the script. So convinced are we that no one would tolerate our presence if they knew what thoughts we harbored, we play hail-fellow, well-met and withhold criticism of our friends' unsavory pastimes. Now our family is the audience. Even backstage, we wear a patina of stubborn greasepaint, lecturing our children on the dangers of the siren song of immoderation, while hiding the wrinkles formed by our disregard of good judgment.

What is wrong with a little bit of let's pretend? Why not don the mask of strength or wisdom or heartiness? Isn't it possible that the act could become father to the thought?

It is possible. That's what rote training used to be all about. Do it often enough and it becomes part of you. The rub is that it doesn't work in the area of human relationships, Dale Carnegie notwithstanding. The heart has its secrets; one of them is the knowledge of authentic love. Your heart is a most sensitive organ, so tender that it can tell whether you are loved for what you really are or for the role you are playing. If the boss loves your flattery, your friends appreciate your tacit approval of their peccadilloes, and your children respect your self-righteousness, your heart knows that the love, appreciation and respect are not for you but for the character you are playing. The hypocrite's fate is to be confronted daily with fondness he can't trust, praise he can't believe, and compassion he can't accept. Each day he pays dearly for gifts he must leave at the theater until he can bear to let the Lord shine the spotlight of truth on his interior life.

There is no better remedy for hypocrisy than prayer before a crucifix. The awful reality of the way Jesus died brings us to our senses, clears our inner vision. The scandal of his nakedness moves impostors to shed pretense and see themselves reduced to bone and flesh and gasping breath. As the Son of God hangs powerless, pinioned by the might of empire and sanctimony, we focus the inner eye upon our sad charade. Still, it is hard to let go. While the truth beneath our precious playacting is indeed riveting, we continue to covet the world's approval. Even as Jesus allows envious men to tear away what they assume to be the last vestige of his honor, you and I cling to hired finery, sequined masks, and fake fur purchased with the currency of deceit. Our costumes fetch a high price, the tender of our self-respect.

The crucifix is a stark reminder of the futility of fashioning a life to fool the crowd. "For if these things are done when the wood is green, what will happen when it is dry?" (Lk 23:31). If the life of the most honest of men came to such a shocking resolution, how will poseurs end? Better that someone warn the emperor that he has no clothes lest his shame be revealed to those whose opinions buttress his exaggerated importance. Here, before the crucifix, we pray that the warning may come from within before we stand at the throne of God as obvious charlatans.

Our prayer is not only that we see ourselves as God sees us, but that we might remedy the false impression presented to the world. It is not enough to kneel at the foot of that honest cross and admit our counterfeit; after all, the Father's eye always pierces the veneer of self-aggrandizement. We also plead for the courage to bring more sincerity to our relationships. Since our conceits led others to react to a pose, our reclaimed openness must transform their estimation of us. And when the image we project comes closer to the truth, those who deal with us will begin to revise their self-evaluations in order to adjust to this new person in their presence. One woman or man struggling for authenticity in the midst of a troupe of masquers is a bright stone hurled into a muddy pond. Rippling honesty eventually scrubs the littered shore.

Even as Truth was nailed to rough wood, his prophetic

ministry continued; his tormentors unknowingly raised a mirror to humankind. No vanity can withstand that image of humility, no sham can find comfort in that reflection of self-effacing love. Each of us would do well to face that mirror often. Prayer before the crucifix reveals who we are and what we should be. There is the emperor with no clothes yet dignified by truth, there is the servant stripped of worldly regard yet crowned with glory.

The actor's life is not for me,
   though all the world's a stage.
      Too dear the time spent making up,
        too small the player's wage
         of thin applause and puffery.
           So now I pledge to God
             to rub the greasepaint from my face
             and leave the boards untrod.

The pose, the witty dialogue
   endeared me to the crowd,
      but seldom did an honest word
        escape my lips aloud.
         To take that final bow, O LORD,
          I must rely on you
            to help me learn just one more line:
             To thine own self be true.
   Amen.

It Took a Mile
to Stop the Mail

At that time, some people who were present there told [Jesus] about the Galileans whose blood Pilate had mingled with the blood of their sacrifices. He said to them in reply: "Do you think that because these Galileans suffered in this way they were greater sinners than all other Galileans? By no means! But I tell you, if you do not repent, you will all perish as they did. Or those eighteen people who were killed when the tower at Siloam fell on them—do you think they were more guilty than everyone else who lived in Jerusalem? By no means! But I tell you, if you do not repent, you will all perish as they did" (Lk 13:1-5).

Too longs, a short, and a long pulled at slumbering townsfolk. The low moan of a whistle from way down the river meant a ghostly freight was hugging the valley walls, keeping out of harm's way, trying to get the scent of the night mail train. The mail would be out there somewhere, highballing from the north, moving so smoothly that men could stand up in the cars and toss into pigeonholes letters flashing like bowie knives hurled at a stump. Nine cars with silver sides slithering down the river on rails greased with four-in-the-morning dew, drawn by a steamer with just a trace of smoke from the stack and a hundred gears working in a blur. They said it took a mile to stop her.

The freight engine was a rusty 2-8-2 with a cowcatcher bent 12 different ways from more than its share of logs and hay wagons and deer taken at the leap. The men in the cab knew the mail was due. But back at the little depot where they had left five flats and a tanker, the sleepy agent called the dispatcher, who said the silversides was running 20 minutes late. The agent didn't wait to hear the explanation. The freight had just pulled out. He slammed down the phone while Dispatch was talking about some troubles with the Limited. He ran a ways up the platform, but the freight was clanking into the tunnel, so he came back to the office and set the three upriver lights in his district from yellow to red. They were sure to see the lights as they pulled into the coulee siding at 4:15. That was when they usually met the mail. He got Dispatch back on the horn and was told tersely that the Capital City Limited, making up three hours after a block at a rockslide, had overtaken the mail at Sommerton. He hung up and began to pray.

The brakeman had barely closed the siding switch after the clattering caboose when he heard the insistent whistle scouring the valley. He looked up at the conductor on the back platform.

"Whitey Hoffman must have left the throttle wide open."

"I don't think it's Whitey. He wouldn't let go of the handle like that."

In less than a minute, the great engine was upon them, spewing staccato shafts of steam at the ballast, sending the stones flying.

"I knew that couldn't be Whitey," hollered the conductor. "It ain't even the mail!"

The beige and green cars swept by, all windows but only a few alight at this early hour. The bull's eye on the back of the observation car fled rapidly down the river—Capital City Limited—then blinked out around a bend.

"That's Shavers!" The brakeman spoke too loudly in the resumed quiet. "He must be three hours late. Somebody musta done a lot of shoveling. I'll bet the rain loosened up. . . ."

Bad news cut him off. It was delivered second by second, car by car as the engine took up the slack in 54 couplings.

"My God," screamed the conductor, "the fool's putting us back on the main! He thought that was the mail!"

He grabbed the brakeman's hand and hoisted him on the

platform, then lurched inside and pulled the caboose's whistle. It was pitifully weak, energized by brake pressure at the end of a long train; they could hardly hear it themselves. The train slowed to let the brakeman close the switch after it had cleared. He moved to his work automatically, then stood there between the rails staring at the shattered stop signal. The hundred little dents on the reflecting collar said shotgun pellets. He didn't move as the conductor met his eyes and nodded. Who jumps back on the Titanic?

Up in the engine cab, both men were busy with the work of getting up to speed. Their noses weren't out for the mail; she had passed. The fireman worked the auger, building the blaze, encouraging the steam. The engineer watched the steep sides of the hills for rain-loosened boulders. Neither saw the fusee's glare from the caboose or the silhouette that jumped clear, then tumbled to the water's edge. Nor did they feel the slight tug of the intermittent braking on the hindmost cars after the conductor had pulled the emergency cord. The serpentine path of the tracks along this river always made it feel as if the last half of any train was dragging its trucks over the ties.

Long-neglected foliage obscured the second red signal, but the engineer saw the third a mile farther on just before the bridge.

"Look, Jack," he cried over the roar of the unchecked locomotive, "a red. You think it's right?"

Without waiting for an answer, he grabbed the brake handle, for even while Jack was saying, "I dunno," the engineer had seen across the short, curved trestle the silver sides of the mail. The distance was not even enough to blur the sparks shooting from her locked wheels. He seemed to be able to count each twinkling little star as it met its mate thrown from the rigid drivers of his own engine. It took a mile to stop the mail, but not this dewy morning.

How many of the nine wives who got calls later that day from the division trainmaster or the district postmaster turned their eyes to heaven and screamed, "God, why did you do this to me?" How many of the 21 men in the hospital at Blue Lake wondered what they had done to deserve their broken limbs, to be caught in the carnage and hear the cries of the dying?

In his book, *When Bad Things Happen to Good People,* Rabbi Harold Kushner says that we can either believe God is all-powerful or that he is all-loving, but the fact of human tragedy keeps us from holding both tenets at the same time. He concludes that God loves us with an infinite love, but is less than all-powerful to the degree that people suffer. This is where Rabbi Kushner differs from traditional Christian thought. Few moderns would assert that God deliberately made widows of those wives or broke the bones of the survivors, but most Christians would say that he simply chose not to tie up all the loose ends in the series of mistakes, perverse decisions, selfish choices and acts of good will that stopped the mail in much less than a mile. God, indeed, is omnipotent, but from time to time he himself limits the use of his power to see if you and I can come to a better, a more free, a more human solution. Many times we do. That night, when the yellow cones of two headlights merged into one, we didn't.

The mail and the freight could have made it to their terminals the next morning if God had used his power to stop some rocks from sliding, to prompt a freight agent to make an earlier call, to convince the foreman of a tree trimming crew to forego his nightly binge, to keep some boys two weeks earlier from emptying their guns at a semaphore, to inspire a manufacturing executive 17 years before to eschew profit in favor of safety in approving a revolutionary brake design for long trains. This list of interventions is infinite. The crews of all three trains, and the mail sorters on the silversides, and all the passengers on the Limited could have suspended their yearning or responsibility to be somewhere else before their fateful journey began and, by giving in to the infinite wisdom and power of God, decided instead to remain where they were that night of whistles and sparks. It could have happened that way for with God, all things are possible. But not all things are probable. The Creator and Sustainer of the universe could have stopped all these journeys before they started, but he chose not to, perhaps to see what these incarnate spirits called women and men could do. Some didn't make it home; upon them the God of infinite love poured his compassion and pretended he didn't hear those who cursed him for his meanness.

Too many of us come to prayer believing every good thing anyone ever told us about God . . . and then some. To the classical attributes of divinity—God is omniscient, omnipresent, omnipotent, all loving, all merciful, all just—we add private beliefs that are really demands, those things that must be true if we are to escape today's particular mess. God must not be bound by the law of contradiction when the gourmand asks his help in shedding 30 pounds while the microwave shorts out from the strain of keeping up. God must break free of the laws of thermodynamics when the procrastinator prays for a warm house after neglecting to pay the January heating bill. The Almighty must be divinely ignorant of the law of supply and demand when the die-hard prays that a publisher will accept her book of Latin hymns. In lifting our minds and hearts to God, we can easily approach that fine line between optimism and irrationality. Now and then, even the most sophisticated Christian will cross that line to become a prayerful Pollyanna.

There is a difference between praying and wishing. Wishing compares a rosy dream of the future to the gray of today; the standard of comparison is what I think is best. In this way I participate in the sin of Adam and Eve. They coveted the attributes of God so as to improve their lot even in the middle of Eden. They would set the standards and the Creator would conform. It didn't wash; they were ushered toward reality at the point of a fiery sword.

Unfortunately, it often takes a fiery sword to point out reality to modern-day wishers who fall on their knees and call it praying. In the hardest cases, self-deceived Christians may sour on prayer altogether, even though they weren't really praying. They might even lose faith in the God who wouldn't answer their "prayers," that is, grant their wishes. Others, however, manage through painful experience to see the folly of their ways. After a time, perhaps a lifetime, of confusing God with a Fairy Godmother, after a series of heartwrenching collisions with reality, the more discerning practitioners of prayer-as-wishful-thinking learn from their mistakes. With due respect for the insight of Rabbi Kushner, they conclude not that God is less than all-powerful or all-loving but that another, very important divine attribute has been overlooked: God is unknowable. This is a shattering admission for anyone who thinks of the Almighty as Superman: a lot like us but more so. In an age in which the image of God as permissive *paterfamilias* is cultivated, there is a refreshing frankness in recognizing God as unrecognizable. If that idea causes fear, it is the holy fear necessary for a healthier, more reasoned spiritual life; it is the fear that is the beginning of wisdom. Wisdom knows what it doesn't know. Wisdom prays to God as absolutely Other. Wisdom relies completely on Divine Providence. Wisdom does not wish for what might be but makes the best of what is.

Almighty God,
    I pray not that you hear me,
        for you hear me even in my silence.
    I ask not that you forgive me,
        for you forgive me even in my failing.

I seek not your revelation,
> for your revelation is my being.
I propose no saving plan,
> for your saving plan is my life.
I protest not your will in this matter,
> for your will is my redemption.
I simply open my heart to your love,
> for my heart is your love.
>> Amen.

The Snake Charmer

On that day, as evening drew on, [Jesus] said to them, "Let us cross to the other side." Leaving the crowd, they took him with them in the boat just as he was. And other boats were with him. A violent squall came up and waves were breaking over the boat, so it was already filling up. Jesus was in the stern, asleep on a cushion. They woke him and said to him, "Teacher, do you not care that we are perishing?" He woke up, rebuked the wind, and said to the sea, "Quiet! Be still!" The wind ceased and there was great calm. Then he asked them, "Why are you terrified? Do you not yet have faith?" They were filled with great awe and said to one another, "Who then is this whom even wind and sea obey?" (Mk 4:35-41).

The river sprang toward the ocean like a rattler uncoiling in mid-strike. It hissed as it reared back on itself, slithering through the heart of the city, making east and west step away from their banks in fear of attracting its attention. A great brown snake it was, barely tolerating the tiny ferry boats that sped across its back. Every now and then when the water was high, it would ripple a muscle and toss a fragile hull, smashing a ferry against the wharves, making people sit up and take notice.

You never forgot the river no matter how many times you crossed. Liquid power seethed around the pilings, fought a churning battle against the first progress of the boat. As you grew older, your caution became more perfunctory, but the fear was always present because you knew things had happened more than once, terrible things that made the headlines. You could never really let yourself go, never enjoy the afternoon's respite from the push and shove of the land as the stevedores did on their way home from work each day. Grizzled men cavorted like schoolboys, stealing one another's lunch boxes, doubling up over a joke, dancing a step or two to a jazzy harmonica.

You could never get into that kind of mood, and it wasn't just because of your color. Hadn't you, for a fact, been invited on one occasion to take a hand of greasy cards in what some of these men called poker? You couldn't do that, shook your head and turned to face the spray at the bow. You heard the remark that followed; you were supposed to. But the dealer was wrong. It wasn't your sense of place that chained you to the rail. It was that brown snake pulling you and your companions away from the farther shore, forcing you little by little from the accustomed route, carrying you toward the mouth of the river, to the edge of the sea.

Halfway across and a slight shudder overcame you. Always you knew when there was less time to come than had been traversed. Nothing changed outwardly. The dockworkers chewed their dead cigars with the same benign rhythm, the engine chugged on doggedly, the propellers kept up the fight. The signal was inside you, a slight shift of perspective and a chill around the heart. The people on the dock at the Point were now bigger than those you left behind. The crisis, if there were to be one, had a smaller window in which to occur. The snake had less time to prove that you were completely in its power. You always wondered if others felt that subtle shift and sharp chill at midpoint. The stevedores seemed caught up in their horseplay, but now did they look as one man to the south? The three prim matrons on the wooden bench outside the cabin wall . . . did they stop chattering at this moment and bend down to touch the tingling deck? You could just see up above the back of the captain's blue coat. Did it suddenly sag then straighten? Who else here in the middle of the brown current felt the coils tighten?

They say when you sneeze you come closest to death because every one of your necessary functions stops. That's how you always felt at midstream. There wasn't enough time for your whole life to pass before your eyes, but the mounting pressure of the contending currents squeezed out of your day the bile of rancor and regret, the residue of your petty offenses against man and God. You usually noticed a metallic taste in your mouth as if you had kissed the brass rail that encircled the deck. It was the taste of remorse come too late, all you had left if, indeed, the snake's hold could not be broken.

You are here today because the hold had always been broken. The mouth of the river at the edge of the sea is not the final resting place for your bones because Someone had charmed the great brown snake, distracted it from the all-too-easy task of pulling your little boat south. The Snake Charmer diverted your captor with other challenges, persuading the slippery serpent that you and the poker players and the chatty ladies were unworthy of its cosmic striving. Each afternoon at mid-river, God tempted the devil with ''all the kingdoms of the world in their magnificence'' (Mt 4:8), mocking Satan's weakness before the fidelity of his beloved Son. And every day, he fell for it, loosening his coiled strength to forage for a more appropriate prey than you.

Each of us crosses a great brown river every day. No matter who we are or pretend to be, we find ourselves in the coils of evil. It twines itself around our good intentions and chokes them into submission, it slips through the gaps between preachment and practice to make hypocrites of us all, it draws us southward to the Tropic of Cancer, to the lush life where temptation labors not. Yet, though it is subtle, the evil of the day cannot completely control each of its rippling muscles. Too often, it throbs in impatience before the final constriction. At midstream the matrons reach down and feel through the deck the pulse of its pride. The dock gang looks to the south to calculate how far off course they've been pulled. The captain lets himself be drawn toward the depths. And you react with a shudder to the force that is crushing you. This is the moment that you must cry out to saving power. You cannot match the devil in subtlety, in strength or in cunning. This is no time for fine points of theology. You have felt the raw pride of evil and know precisely where the current has already taken you. Terrible things have happened before, things that made the headlines. Your prayer is simple, heartfelt and absolutely self-centered: "God, help me!"

God is the Snake Charmer. Two thousand years ago, the world taught him that so long as he tolerated the continued existence of humankind, he could not finally conquer evil. He could win a battle on a Sunday morning in Jerusalem, but Herod would sin again on Monday. So each day God plays on his pipes to attract the snake's attention just for a moment, enough time to free you, to permit you to resume your journey to the other shore. Someday, perhaps, the Snake Charmer will tire of this game and allow the coils of evil to writhe uncontrolled and carry this presumptious people to the vaults of the deep sea. That day will not come, however, as long as there is left one man or woman to reach down and touch the tingling deck, to feel the pulse of deep water roiling, to tremble at the power of evil and cry in unabashed selfishness: "God, help me!"

"But deliver us from evil." So we conclude our hurried *Pater,* tearing through the last of it like a buzz saw at the end of a plank. Daily bread and trespasses catch our attention; we know what we need and we know what we've done, but the evil out there waiting for us gets barely a nod. This tendency to minimize the threat of lurking calamity is the hallmark of an age of positive thinking. Dread is passé: You, there, shivering in your shoes, are simply a victim of free-floating anxiety. I know a psychologist who can help you.

It does seem old-fashioned, perhaps even un-American, to see a malign force behind each tree. In a society in which every day, in every way, things are getting better and better, the emphasis must be on progress. That which impedes progress is analyzed, diagnosed, therapeutically demythologized. Haven't the mavens of mental health certified that only the guilt-ridden hesitate as they conjure up their private *bêtes noires?*

The praying person knows better, knows that the powers of darkness have not been in hibernation these past two thousand years. Chastened by the brevity of its triumph on Calvary, evil lowered its sights and has been content to play havoc with mere men and women ever since. The strategy is simple: Lie low among the cockeyed optimists. Convince them that they stand on the threshold of Utopia. Then, pull the rug out from under them.

"Deliver us from evil" is a most unsophisticated prayer. It says of the praying person that he or she has good reason to be afraid, that there are things beyond human control, that neither hurricane nor heartache is amenable to reasoned argument. Evil personified in madman or wanton cares nothing for intelligent discourse. Mindless mayhem is countered only by a higher order, namely, the compassionate plan of God. "Deliver us from evil" is the prayer of the child in a thunderstorm, the woman in the oncology ward, the man in the falling plane. It is faith speaking, not science; trust rather than positive thinking. It is a humbling prayer that forces us to admit our powerlessness. Too bad Jesus didn't make it the first line of the Our Father, for it tells us precisely who we are and whom we need.

We rattle along,
        prattling on
                of Rorschach and enneagrams,
                bumping into mismatched forebears,
                neurotic nurses, prisoned ids,
                in search of hidden villainy.
                        While you wait, LORD.
                        While you wait.

99

We patter along,
    scattering on
        our loyal, luckless coterie
        dainty darts of accusation,
        sophisticated estimates
        of where it all turned upside down.
           While you wait, LORD.
           While you wait.

We battle along,
    shattered upon
        our dark, demanding reveries,
        yearning for becalmed perfection,
        in search of that cerebral sword
        to slay the goblins of the night.
           While you wait, LORD.
           While you wait.

We chatter along,
    nattering on
        of self-affirming strategies,
        when one day all logic crumbles,
        some shock which forces us to plead
        with empty hands upraised and hope
           it's not too late, LORD.
           Not too late?
           Amen.

Autumn Leaves

Jesus answered them, "The hour has come for the Son of Man to be glorified. Amen, amen, I say to you, unless a grain of wheat falls to the ground and dies, it remains just a grain of wheat; but if it dies, it produces much fruit. Whoever loves his life loses it, and whoever hates his life in this world will preserve it for eternal life" (Jn 12:23-25).

Thick socks always meant hiking. You began to feel different as soon as you bent to the bottom drawer and took in the faint smell of bluing. Clean socks for a clean break. And serious boots with leather laces to bind the promise made to you this morning by the tree outside your window. "It's here," whispered the elm, shyly lifting a dozen green leaves to show their yellowing bellies. Last night, a chill hand had caressed the trees, urging them to mark what was coming. It was the signal to begin to withdraw from the lush season, to recall from extremities the verdant life that thickened shiny leaves.

At the back of the closet you found the weathered mop handle so dear since that time it flipped the snake into the stream. You took a couple of bills from your wallet and left it on the dresser as confirmation of this day's detachment from licenses, addresses—anything that could tie you to the pretense of routine, keep you from the mountain's bittersweet revelations. This was a day for looking at past and future, for a bold trek into autumn, that deceptive season that once again promised to tell you the truth.

The promise would be kept. You parked the car at the old ranger station after using every bit of your resolve to keep from being hypnotized by the riotous display while you drove. You wouldn't look at it until you had climbed the ladder to the first level of the tower. Only when you rested on the tiny platform would you let your eyes sweep along the worn hills surrounding the cloud-capped peak. Before you was spread not only the portrait of a season but the spectrum of your life as it was and as it would be. Blood red were the oaks, painted with vital oils, profligate with the hot blood of youth. There, yellow and orange gowns wantonly displayed, bare-shouldered in the bloom of life, poking an insouciant elbow in the eye of inevitability. The poplars were gold, regal, haughty with the satisfaction of middle age and deserved success, bending condescendingly in the wind over their sisters still green and envious. A patchwork canopy of crimson and pink and rose and bronze and magenta and beige invited you to descend and wander in a life well-lived. Only when your eyes finally beheld what drove Van Gogh mad did you come down to begin the second half of your journey. You came down to face the truth.

You could not avoid the truth as you walked through the fallen leaves under that vivid array that danced in the breeze and made the sky a washed-out blue. Every step spoke its name. Each time you put your foot upon a great flaming maple leaf, it cracked. It broke. It shattered with a snap. The truth was brittle; there clung to it the smell of the bonfire. All this, so beautiful when glimpsed from afar, was death's doing.

This truth was curled and cramped like a maimed hand, incapable of holding on to the branch when autumn's astringent breath whispered in the crisp dawn. Detachment followed, the severing of the last hope of knowing the stream of life again— detachment, the loss of all caring, of any union with one who lives. And then the irresistible fall into the decadence foreshadowed by the flamboyant palette. The truth was simply this: This dance of colors, this whirling kaleidoscope was stimulated not by an infusion of life but by its exact opposite.

Always, as you walked out of the woods, you would carry with you three or four of the most beautiful leaves, vowing to preserve them somehow from winter's constricting power. A leaf is such a fragile thing to begin with. Even in the sinewy green of summer, a sudden storm will tear it from the branch. Later, when days grow short, a special reverence is required to preserve a bit of the brittle canvas. Try as you may, you were not able even once to bring home an integral leaf. The bounce of the car, the pressure of your fingers snapped the vein, crushed the parchment. In those days you were too clumsy to preserve life.

Now, you know better the cost of conservation. You have learned that there are so many things you don't know, so many uncertainties supporting mere endurance. In matters pertaining to your continued existence, you have had to acquire the delicate touch. Life can, indeed, be enjoyed, can be clothed with the bright colors of friendship and celebration, but all this with deliberation. Foresight and circumspection are the watchwords when handling something as fragile as a dry leaf, a flag still bright, bravely unfurled in the wind of time, but no longer leading the parade.

You have learned also that it is wrong to remember the brilliant carpet on the forest floor as a sign of despair. At one time, you may have sadly tramped those woods in the knowledge that each footfall simply hurried the inevitable. What was inevitable then was annihilation, the black abyss born of the superstitions of elders and your own terrifying nightmares. Today, you are more convinced than ever that death is as inevitable as the falling leaves. You have seen it happen to a friend or family member; it has touched you, chilled you, but not overpowered you. Even more than inevitable, death has now become for you necessary. One day, perhaps, it will become a friend.

In John's gospel, Jesus tells us that there is no rising without dying. The grain of wheat, the golden leaf, must fall to the ground. That blanket of leaves which so often saddened you became each winter a coverlet protecting the first stirrings of new life. With the spring rain, it was transformed to rich, fecund soil, new earth nurturing new life. Each flash of crimson and canary gave up its glow to make a warm matrix for resurrection.

No one seeks the agony of death. Even Jesus asked that the cup of suffering be taken from him. But he knew as you have learned that death must come if the transformation of our earthly lives into glory is to be accomplished. Yes, autumn can be a melancholy season, swept by the memories of a more vital time. We would be less than human if a touch of sadness did not come with the chilly wind. But the Christian's trust in the promise of everlasting life, and in that one life given as proof of the promise, permeates these dwindling days with warm hope and swirling flames of yellow and orange. They will dance once more before they fall to dust.

The adventure of growing old is a fertile field for prayer. Those who do not see the process of aging as an adventure keep their petitions simple and direct, something on the order of "Rescue me." They seek the Lord's help in being preserved from the rigors of illness, loneliness, forgetfulness. While these are surely cries from the heart, they betray a lack of confidence in the continuum of life so strikingly revealed in the resurrection. In his escape from the tomb, Christ summoned from the 30 years of his earthly life the treasure of trust burnished and purified in his many sufferings. That fidelity to his Father's will became the essence of his new life. This should come as no surprise, since the gospels reveal that trust was the guiding force of his ministry.

To the extent that we trust God here, so shall we find that trust affirmed hereafter. That confidence brings joy to any life in this world, and especially to that of the later years. If we go looking for troubles, we shall find them; but if we rely on the One who makes all things new, we shall find his transforming love in any situation, no matter how outwardly oppressive. The process of aging, when suffused with trust in God's providential care, not only can but must be an adventure.

The dictionary defines adventure as a risky undertaking. The confident Christian counting the years sees it differently. Her prayer or his is not for rescue but for revelation, for the chance to see the many colors of divine love that play across the autumn landscape: the pink smile of a grandchild, the faintly purple joke with an old friend, the silvery tinkle of easy conversation with a loyal spouse, the multi-hued movement of a solemn liturgy, the gold of ready companionship in times of trial. Simple things? Indeed, too simple for the young to understand, but simple things are all that really matter to the person relying not on mental acuity or physical prowess, but only on God.

Adventure in the autumn is not only possible but necessary to avoid the incremental suicide of just waiting for the end. Our prayer should not be to prevent the falling of the grain of wheat to the earth. It must fall, and it will. Our prayer, rather, is that in the slow descent, we might let go of the spindly structure of self-salvation and let ourselves be borne upward again and again in the warm breeze of God's love. The waiting earth will receive us soon enough, but if we trust in him who makes all things new, oh, how many little glories in the going.

So many days we've wasted, Lord,
upon the quest to weave a life,
to fashion from the threads of time
and circumstance a tapestry
incorporating equal strands
of piety and self-concern
offending neither Maker nor
the world's severe criteria.
At sunset, standing back to view
the grand design, we see it come
unraveled at the interlace,

deficient in the tie that binds—
that certain trust in Providence
which holds the years together—and
in humble genuflection ask
that you would work the loom anew.
       Amen.

Man's Best Friend

Where can I go from your spirit?
　　from your presence where can I flee?
If I go up to the heavens, you are there;
　　if I sink to the nether world,
　　　　you are present there.
If I take the wings of the dawn,
　　if I settle at the farthest limits of the sea,
Even there your hand shall guide me,
　　and your right hand hold me fast.
If I say, ''Surely the darkness shall hide me,
　　and night shall be my light''—
For you darkness itself is not dark,
　　and night shines as the day (Ps 139:7-12).

"So black, he's blue!" That's what the country woman said of him. She had just moved with four skinny kids into the old Bartlett house across the alley, bringing with her a well-stocked store of oblique wisdom—maxims and saws that immediately cast her in the role of rustic oracle. Back on the farm, you supposed, there was no hint of the adept in her monosyllables. There, the folks were all laconic Platos; here, you had to decipher even her comment about your dog. You had to go outside and look at him, which wasn't easy because he didn't like being observed as something separate from you. It wasn't in his nature to tolerate distance between you and him except for a very few, mutually acceptable reasons: If you drove away in the car or put him in the basement or turned and told him "Stop!" before you crossed the street, he assumed it was for his own good. Acts so dramatic must have their bases in love or hate; he always presumed the former. But to expect him to remain curled up under a tree while you sat 30 feet away watching him from a lawn chair . . . well he knew better than that. This wasn't the basement or the driveway or the street corner. His place was at your side, where he promptly took himself.

So you tried to observe him from four inches. There was no arguing his blackness. The telltale white of old age around his jowls simply heightened the contrast. But his fervid panting and imploring whine made it awfully hard to think philosophically. You relented, took his head into your lap and massaged his ears. It wasn't until that night when you let him out for his visit to the apple tree that you saw, or better, didn't see, and understood. As you stepped to the kitchen door, the kids made some commotion upstairs that called forth your warning thrown back into the house. When you turned again to the cool night, he was gone.

Your eyes followed the beam from the light over the garage door to the shadowed corner of the yard. The basement door was closed. The hole in the fence remained mended. You were about to step out to make a wider search when you caught just a whiff of the familiar odor, his smell. Turning, you found him sitting behind you, tongue lolling, forepaw upraised for the customary handshake, the goodbye you always exchanged before his nightly business trip. It was the required proof that you would wait for him. You had forgotten it that evening and he was waiting.

That time, you kept your eye on him as he snuffled at the lawn mower, briskly reconnoitered the garage, finally stopped at the tree, and scratched up a little grass afterward. How many times before had you really seen him at night—nights when you were worried about the payments on the car or about the war, nights when your heart flew on love's wings to the sparkling stars? You shook his paw and he disappeared. So black, he was blue. So black, he hid in the night. So black, he went right through black to another color, another dimension. This dog that loved you so became obediently invisible when your focus changed. He showed himself to you at your wish, put his head up or down, extended his paw, rolled over, nuzzled your hand, all at your command. When your ardor waned, he faded into the night, though still on his

108

rounds, still protecting you, guarding you, panting with love for you, waiting unseen, waiting for you to come to your senses, to choose loyalty over diversion, a sure thing over a high flier.

It wasn't just at the dinner table that he loved you. Your absent-minded gift of gristle was very much appreciated, of course; even as he chewed, he had his eye on you. He was loyal to the other you as well. When you were beastly, he forgave you; when his water was dirty, he trusted you to notice; when he howled in the cold rain while you had your feet up before the fire, he understood even as he cried in regret over your disloyalty. Sometimes, your punishments were beyond his endurance; a feral growl escaped his clenched teeth despite his efforts to muzzle the fearsome power of righteousness. He was at his best on the long walks, scouting the territory, standing point, routing the woodchuck, barking for the sheer joy of protecting you from a world of danger to which you were oblivious.

You were oblivious to so much of what he did for you, the chances he took, the ogres he battled even in his sleep. The nightmares that made him rumble and shake were shadowed scenes of impending doom from which he saved you again and again. You did not often reward his constancy, yet he was content to live for those infrequent words of praise that made him scamper and sneeze. He was not embarrassed at the paroxysm of happiness that shook him from nose to tail from simply seeing you bend down and slap your hand against your knee. Mostly, though, he was invisible; so black, he was blue; so steady in his uncritical estimation of your virtues that you never saw him for what he was: the hound of heaven.

If all creatures reflect the wisdom of their maker, then the world and its denizens taken together form a portrait of God. Each animal can be said to give its unique witness to a facet of divine being. From lowly slug to soaring eagle, the attributes of the Creator shine forth. That which sparkles in the snapping eye of a dog is loyalty, a quiet faithfulness, a willingness to remain invisible until invited into our plans. Recall in prayer those situations in which God was farthest from your mind, yet watching over you with love. It might have been a season of despair or a day of peril. Not until the crisis ended and you sensed the power he had wielded in your behalf did you think to yourself, "God must have been so close and I didn't realize it." He was there, so black, he was blue; ignored or taken for granted or purposely shut out, his love was steady, his protection sure.

Most of us, however, do not live in constant crisis. The quiet march of uneventful days tends to retard the process of remembrance. After all, what is there in the inconsequential worth recalling? Just that: the paring knife that didn't slip, the step-stool that didn't collapse. It seems an odd use of memory, remembering little things that didn't happen: the long night drive when your eyes stayed open, the slip on the stairs when you caught your balance, the forgotten bathtub with the overflow drain that worked. Instead of complaining about the humdrum, one should pause now and then to ponder the providence that allows easy routine. With the lidded eye of prayer, we see that God is before and behind us, taking the point, protecting us against picayune perils we shall never know. Even when we flee him "down the nights and down the days," he is there, silent, watchful, brooding upon our welfare, sensitive to a shift in the wind or a shift in the earth. Unseen and uncomplaining, he waits for some simple acknowledgment, some hurried thank you. Yet, even without a sign of appreciation, he will be constant and loyal in his love. He will forgive our ingratitude.

God's loyalty to you is defined by his willingness to forgive. He will pardon your indifference and neglect, forget yesterday's betrayals as he walks by your side, pleased to be invited again into your world . . . until the next time you make a mess of things, until the next time the merciless wheels of circumstance threaten to grind you up, until the next time you leave the iron on during your favorite soap opera. Know and take solace in the assurance that he will be waiting in the corner of your shadowed world, so black, he is blue, invisible in the darkness of your soul, steady in his love, ready for your call.

We are not a faithless people, LORD,
    just humble folks too proud to beg.
        Enamored of our wits,
        encumbered by our woes,
        we simply choose to work it out
            apart from *force majeure.*
        Why engage the molder of mountains
          to fortify a molehill?

We are not the czars of destiny
    ordained to lead some great crusade,
        proclaim the end of want
        or cleanse the world of hate.
        Our sorrows are so commonplace,
          our joys of little weight
        matched against galactic upheavals
          contending for your notice.

We are rapt observers of the Christ,
    bedazzled by his miracles,
        preoccupied by might
        and raging seas made calm,
        while overlooking fields ablaze
          in raiment fit for kings,
        sparrows borne on high by his Spirit,
          and children finding kindness.

We are not a faithless people, LORD,
    but please increase our willingness
        to seek your daily grace,
        that constant involvement
        with ev'ry creature of the earth
            revealed when your own Son
        squandered all to live with the lowborn
            and join us in our struggle.
                Amen.

A String of Pearls

In the sixth month, the angel Gabriel was sent from God to a town of Galilee called Nazareth, to a virgin betrothed to a man named Joseph, of the house of David, and the virgin's name was Mary. And coming to her, he said, "Hail, favored one! The LORD is with you." But she was greatly troubled at what was said and pondered what sort of greeting this might be. Then the angel said to her: "Do not be afraid, Mary, for you have found favor with God. Behold, you will conceive in your womb and bear a son, and you shall name him Jesus. He will be great and will be called Son of the Most High, and the LORD God will give him the throne of David his father, and he will rule over the house of Jacob forever, and of his kingdom there will be no end" (Lk 1:26-33).

Sister Bernardine's rosary moved to her many moods. When she was agitated, it was the chain on a grandfather clock, hoisted and tightened and lowered and loosened on her brown cincture. She wound it up and let it go, ticking off the crimes of the classroom. As she hurried purposefully through the halls, it hung straight down, steady, deliberate, plumblike against the frenzied movement of her barely discernible limbs. Yet, when she was at rest, sitting on the high stool behind her raised desk, her beads became a pendulum. Some magnetic power at the earth's core made the crucifix swing in a shallow arc, just the distance from doubt to certainty. Many were the students who measured the glacial passage of class time by that unfailing rhythm. Of these and other remarkable configurations of her rosary, Sister was unmindful. The rosary was an instrument of prayer, nothing less, prayer with her sisters before the 6:00 a.m. Mass, prayer alone at 8:00 p.m. before retiring, and prayer at half-past three in the afternoon in Room 206 for those students who had forgotten what school was for. It was in Room 206 that your initial interest in the rosary became a bitter entanglement and sweet boredom turned sour.

Sister Bernardine had the big rosary, the whole thing. Fifteen minutes of 50 Hail Marys would hardly repair the damage you did to scholarly decorum. Sister required nothing less than the rosary that God gave us, all 15 decades, 150 "Aves," as she called them, to keep you prayerfully occupied for seven minutes short of an hour. The Hail Holy Queen and other auxiliary supplications rounded out the 60 minutes. At the public school, so you were told, "staying after" meant a study hall and a head start on homework. Not at St. Luke's. At St. Luke's you prayed.

Sister Bernardine was a progressive educator. St. Luke's was not a concentration camp and the rosary was not an instrument of torture. For the first decade, you expected to kneel: just deserts and all that. Then for the second, you stood. And for the third, you sat, and so on. Kneeling was pure hell, relieved only slightly by the resilience of the board flooring which allowed you to send messages to fellow detainees, squeak by squeak. Standing brought you to eye level with Sister as she corrected papers at her Olympian desk. No room for funny business under her restless gaze. When sitting for the third decade, you could snap shut your desk lid and make a friend click his tongue and snort. Kneeling, however, afforded the opportunity to make a variety of unusual noises as the floor writhed in agony. Unfortunately, your knees and thighs soon writhed in agony. The result of all this sound and fury was always the same. Well before Mary was crowned Queen of Heaven and Earth, you had resolved never again to get yourself into this kind of pickle.

It was a promise with a dull edge. You, of course, visited Room 206 many times in your academic career. The sweet sound of laughter from your classmates was too powerful a lure; you entertained each class that appreciated your comedic talents right up until the day of graduation. The other side of the promise, however, did keep its edge. The last time you left Room 206 was the last time you finished a rosary.

The rosary was a foolish way for a young modern to pray. Was God really more apt to hear 50 Hail Marys than one? And who could concentrate on the words anyway? The repetition numbed the mind, insulted the intellect, and, as you heard from more than one newly-minted priest, was "a-liturgical." Repetition was out; spontaneity was in. Still, you tried the beads on rare occasions in the years since Sister shouted the mysteries, usually when the need to alter your fortunes was critical, when you would stoop to any level to change God's mind. Never once did you make it to the last decade; you could get past the want of logic and even through herculean effort maintain your concentration, but you could not escape the memory of Room 206 where lassitude had turned to distaste and boredom to bile.

Now, in some jumbled drawer lies a coil of beads growing dull with time. Tangled around tarnished Miraculous Medals and yellowed holy cards, a clouded string of pearls waits for the world to turn full circle. You saw it there last when you were searching for your class ring before the reunion; somehow, it had made the trip from the old house to the new. Whatever made you save it as you courageously discarded desiccated ball point pens and grotesque money clips? Into the trash went check stubs, broken combs, suppurating flashlight batteries, and a gnawed Art Gum eraser, but the rosary found its way from pine desk to cherrywood dresser, transplanted hundreds of miles because you weren't sure how to properly dispose of a blessed item. At least, that's what you told yourself as you held above the wastebasket the long-banished beads blinking in surprise at the light. The real reason lies elsewhere, though. You still have that rosary because throwing it away would not get rid of it. It's inside you, has been since Room 206. Sometimes, in a moment of stress or sorrow, you can hear the voices mumbling in adenoidal apathy the latter halves of Our Fathers and Hail Marys, answering the challenge of a small woman in a brown habit, numbering your crimes, totaling your redemption.

It is time to try the beads again. After all these years, it is high time to put your grudges behind you. It was all very well to declare your independence from rote prayer when so many different ways of praying were available. You gave yourself with unchecked enthusiasm to each new suggestion; each was to be the answer to distraction, aridity, boredom. There was spontaneous prayer, roleplaying, the Jesus prayer, guided imagery, the desert experience. How many mantras did you memorize? You stood with arms raised, sat with legs twined, lay flat on your back. Each new approach and posture brought a rush of sensitivity to the divine, a feeling of closeness to God, a taste for more intimate union. Always, though, your honeymoon with the Lord was all too brief. Time after time, you gave up on prayer as a medium for perceived grace. Each peak gave way to a long valley of spiritual inactivity.

Pick up the beads again, but leave the painful memories to Sister Bernardine. She has long since passed to her reward and has taken the rosary-as-punishment with her. God has blessed her for her zeal and assigned her to repair any damage she may have inadvertently caused. She kneels beside you now, urging you to understand her motives. Her aim was to teach unruly children the discipline of prayer, to take a simple theme and by repetition cause it to permeate the marrow of their bones. To this extent, and putting aside the resistance you brought to the process, she succeeded. You still know the rosary; after a lifetime of determined neglect, you can pray it in your sleep.

The rosary is a prayer for a distracted age, for a people unsure of the validity of their concourse with divinity. When you finish the rosary, you have accomplished something. You may not feel any closer to God, but you are certain you have honored him. In seek-

ing the intercession of the Blessed Virgin Mary, you have authenti-
cally stretched your horizon by invoking the name and the reputation of one who partakes of glory. The rosary is one antidote to the
occupational hazard that the prayerful Christian describes with the
question: "Have I merely been talking to myself?" No one can ad-
dress the Mother of God 53 times and still ask that question.

Yes, the rosary is anti-modern. In a society mesmerized by
glitz, it has no glamor. It is naiveté in a cunning world. It is plain,
gray flannel against silvery satin and gold lamé. But it works.
When you finish the rosary, no matter how far afield your mind has
wandered, your heart knows you prayed. Holy Mary takes your
plea, gently squeezes out the distractions, and presents it to her
Son. And sainted Sister Bernardine stands up, massages her old
knees, and, smiling beatifically, goes looking for another of her pu-
pils.

I believe in God,
>who heeds the most distracted prayer,
>who sees among the ashes of routine
>a spark of nascent faith
>and welcomes faint beginning,
>the glinting promise of real fire.

Our Father, you are in heaven
>and we are not,
>You are simply single-minded
>and we are not,
>unconstrained by schedules,
>constant in attention,
>pledged to wait for ever
>for a word announcing
>our desire to be
>>what we are not.

117

Lead us not into despairing
of your answer to our plea.
Do deliver us from daring
not to pierce the mystery
of Perfection humbly sharing
imperfection's threnody.

Holy Mary, Mother of God,
        translator of the hurried petition,
        polestar of wandering thoughts,
        harmony beneath the discord of care.
    Gather up the fragments of our pleading
        and make of them a grace-filled song,
        a gift of trust in the Son you bore,
        a noble hymn to the Son you serve.

Glory, glory to Father, Son, and Spirit.
    Garbled glory, yes:
        abstracted alleluias
  heedless hosannas
        scatterbrained psalms
  dreamy doxologies.

Glory, glory to a God
    who hears the mumbled, rumbled pleas,
    who hears and heeds the stumbled pleas,
    who heeds the fumbled pleas
    of fickle folks upon their knees.
        Amen.

Palpable Grace

In the beginning, when God created the heavens and the earth, the earth was a formless wasteland, and darkness covered the abyss, while a mighty wind swept over the waters.

Then God said, "Let there be light," and there was light. God saw how good the light was. God then separated the light from the darkness. God called the light "day," and the darkness he called "night." Thus evening came, and morning followed—the first day.

Then God said, "Let there be a dome in the middle of the waters, to separate one body of water from the other." And so it happened: God made the dome, and it separated the water above the dome from the water below it. God called the dome "the sky." Evening came, and morning followed—the second day (Gn 1:1-8).

Rain always dampened the spirits of Louella and Rose down at the telephone office. They weren't so quick to ring your house nor were they anxious to get an answer from any of the ladies of the club with whom you had to compare notes. Rain kept the world from your living room. The steady static on the radio drowned out the news from New York and Washington. Automobiles slowed down when it rained; not wishing to dirty their fender skirts, they avoided narrow, poorly drained streets like yours. Rain kept surprise visitors and salesmen from your door, prevented you from being industrious in the garden, cured the cat of wanderlust. Rain kept things from happening. You treasured rainy days.

You knew that golf games were being ruined and kids kept inside at recess. Nylons were getting muddied, newspaper ink was running, streetcars were late, and policemen were soaked to the skin. Not your worry. You had your cup of tea, your book, the phonograph. Above all, you had that gentle sweep of liquid grace upon your roof, cleansing your home and your heart of the stain of care. Spring rain, then, was a welcome baptism purifying your prospects, dissolving the crust of original anxiety that imprisoned hope. If there was acid in it, you hadn't heard.

The cardinal in the budding oak outside your window sang in praise of God's mercy upon the thirsty land. Through the rivulets on the pane, he of the crimson crest seemed operatic, swelling with his heartfelt prayer, striking a pose, arranging the fold of his wings in the midst of a dramatic trill. A singer in the rain, he waved a flashing pennant against the drear sky, carrying in his throbbing throat the only news you wanted to hear: that God had blessed this day and given it to you, that God had muffled the sharp sounds of speed and metal and urgency in order that you might listen to the murmur of creation, that God was pouring out upon the place you called your soul a fresh fall of love from which would spring a hundred pristine hopes, a thousand dreams newborn. The cardinal ended his aria, flexed his moist feathers, and swooped to the Morse's majestic willow, there to include the sorrowing Florence in his circle of intimates. You prayed that she was at her front window to receive the same message: God's compassion is upon this land.

The rumble of the thunder was most polite in adapting itself to your reverie. There may have been lightning somewhere, a writhing stream of ions striking white hot upon a cold bog making the mud sizzle and smoke, but it was hidden from you. All you heard was the pillow-soft concussion of air upon which you rested your thoughts. It was your thunder and you tucked it behind your head against the hard ash of the rocking chair. The rain fell softly, a cushion against the unexpected, a gift from heaven that swept your mind free of self-protective industry; made thus vulnerable, you welcomed the muted crash of power that couldn't harm you. It seemed as though nothing could intrude upon the seamless sound of the rocker squeaking, the cat purring, Toscanini bringing Brahms to life, and, arching over all, a domed firmament porous enough to let God's grace envelop you. Those days when heaven's freshet gentled your soul must surely have stretched back to the Garden and the Creator walking among the dripping leaves to pluck a beaded camellia for Eve's auburn hair.

Today, we are the masters. By our own ingenuity, we have made the rain little more than an inconvenience. Our high-rise apartments and office buildings are impervious to the code of love tapped upon roofs 20 stories above. Gray skies recoil from the megawatt fluorescents in our ceilings. Each hour the weather channel predicts the beginning and end of precipitation with minute-to-minute accuracy. All this technology is directed to a common goal: avoidance. We don't approve of rain precisely because it snarls traffic, disrupts communication, stains the mail; it slows us down. We will not go out in it, we will not suffer being locked in by it, we will not allow our progress to be impeded by it. Stubborn in our disregard, we will not recognize it, will not take the time, will not slow our pace, will not contemplate the symbolic meaning that stretches from Genesis through our treasured memories to this day when data drowns out thunder: Rain is the grace of God made palpable.

Prayer is self-disclosure. Grace is God's appreciation of that revelation. As you describe yourself to him in petition, adoration and thanksgiving, God shows himself in grace. What do you seek today? Strength, hope, forgiveness? What do you offer? Praise, constancy, obedience? You are revealing yourself to be one who wavers and ponders, one who believes and rejoices. Most of us would hesitate to expose our inmost yearnings to our closest friend on earth, but we trust that our best friend in heaven will accept them, and in doing so, accept us whole and entire. All authentic prayer is self-communication. Faith tells us that God responds in kind.

Grace is God's self-communication to us. He does not simply offer a sketch of himself in ancient stories of prophets and patriarchs. He even goes beyond the wondrous likeness revealed in his Son two thousand years ago. In answering our prayers with grace, God offers the ultimate communication; he comes to make his home with us today. Weighty tomes of theology cannot obscure this simple outline of grace: God dwelling among us here, among us now.

God's self-communication is life for the soul; gentle as an April shower, his tender persuasion calls forth a new growth of hope and healing, consolation and serenity, purpose and joy. He sends his grace upon the land and its people, pours out divine nourishment that will not return to him until winter gives way to spring, until fragile shoots are strengthened and the harvest is assured.

Each day can be a day of grace if it is a day of prayer. Each day can be the Lord's day for those who are not afraid to reveal themselves in quiet confidence to the One who waits to console and affirm. Although God sees all that is hidden, he is moved by the self-revelation of his children, moved to prove his love and mercy in the most intimate concourse. He comes to stay with those who pray, to bless with his gentle presence those who lift their heads to feel the freshness of the rain.

A prayer in the rain. It doesn't matter where. A sewing room ablaze with colored remnants. A loft redolent of new-mown hay. A front room overlooking a streaming street. A kitchen with boots piled against the back door. Look outside. See grace falling upon the land, upon its people, upon your parched soul. Hear the song of God on the roof, against the window pane. Feel the shriveled theme of your life absorb his life force. Drink in the dew of blessing. Listen. . . . Spirit calls to spirit, love to love, in the murmur of muted thunder.

Rock-hard, the wintry earth resists
the latent pressure of a seed
about to burst, until a drop
of questing rain responds to need.

Far-fallen did the love of God
explode upon the crusty loam,
then gathered once again to seek
a fissured path to buried home,

and to the grain gave promise sure
of sunlight, nurture, fragile bloom
until, weak reach exceeding grasp,
a shoot escaped from moistened womb.

Surprised, the soil at this new growth;
surprised, my soul at life reborn,
for I was faithless in the cold,
entombed, bound-tight in hope forlorn.

Then, answering persuasive grace
upon my world so gently poured,
I pierced the arid caul of doubt
to blossom and to praise you, Lord.
       Amen.

The Theme Beneath

When John heard in prison about the works of the Messiah, he sent his disciples to him with the question, "Are you the one who is to come, or do we look for another?" Jesus said to them in reply, "Go and tell John what you hear and see: the blind regain their sight, the lame walk, lepers are cleansed, the deaf hear, the dead are raised, and the poor have the good news proclaimed to them. And blessed is the one who takes no offense at me" (Mt 11:2-6).

The trumpets were three blocks long by the time they broke through the din of cicadas in the back yard. Cutting corners, skirting houses, surging down the streets, bursting through the alley, the brassy blast hit you in the back of the head and bounced your eyes off the newspaper. Thursday night. The band concert. There it was on Page Four. Sousa Marches. Glenn Miller Medley. Patriotic Songs. Was that the roll of a drum? Was that "Yankee Doodle"? No more light to read the paper by. The rest of the family had already gone to the park. You had plans for this evening at home, but you hadn't counted on the long reach of the trumpets. A walk, that was the ticket! And if it carried you past the park, no harm done.

By the time you glimpsed the flag on the top of the bandstand, the last of the marches was ending. People were getting up from the rainbow of blankets spread on the slope above the amphitheater, old folks making sure their limbs were locked securely before shifting important weight, kids bouncing up and bolting through the lambent dusk, fathers going back to the car at the curb to get another Coke. Only the teenagers kept an earnest ear on the music as if it were being played just for them. Those who weren't in the band were sitting on running boards—facing the sloping green if they were just friends, facing the street if there was more to it—all listening intently underneath their chatter. You decided not to cross the street, instead took a place with the deputy on the Courthouse steps.

After the military air ended, you could see Mr. Tucker, the band teacher, unleashing a well-honed harangue upon the percussion section. The boys had probably been tapping their sticks on the steel risers during a protracted rest, just as you had done so long ago under the anguished eye of the same Mr. Tucker. As he resumed the dais, the saxophones stood up. "In the Mood" would be rendered very carefully.

Nobody moved to the music in those days, at least not at a band concert on a July evening heavy with parental vigilance. Even the most up-tempo dance tune was played as an exercise to be graded. Family groups on the blankets accepted "Chattanooga Choo Choo" with the same gravity as they had "The Stars and Stripes Forever." The running board kids, however, seemed to hear a different, important message in each selection. While Mr. Tucker—known as "Professor Metronome" for his steady baton—betrayed not a hint of abandon, the young people lounging on the parked cars around the square gave themselves to something else in the music, something other than precision. They strained to hear a voice in the tubas and tympani and trombones, felt an indefinable reverberation deep inside themselves. What was it in this pedantic performance that so mesmerized these kids? For a while, you attempted to concentrate on the whole of what little art was being offered, but soon you were drawn to the private sounds of the Abbott boy's English horn, the Swinkle twins' flutes, the still-unpaid-for clarinet of your own flesh and blood. Suddenly there occurred some convergence of primal tones, an obscure strain deeper than memory which allowed you to hear it: a timid shout of joy, a hesitant proclamation of individuality, of discrete life bursting forth. All at once, each swirl of notes was a flapping banner of hope held not too high behind the staff of discipline. Did the other parents

126

hear it? Did Mr. Tucker feel it slip through the rigid arrangement? These thick-fingered boys and breathless girls were describing in sharps and flats a different world, a land where meaning waited, waited for them.

There it was in Billy Packard's oboe, a low moaning, a longing to break free from petty restrictions. Robbie Walters' blaring trumpet said, "Look at me! I am not my brother, the football hero. I'm me. I am making you wince." Alice Protchek's glockenspiel rang the changes in her life—child, girl, woman—back and forth across 10 years of questions without answers in the space of 16 bars. And what of your own, the clarinet sweeping from blue to red hot? She of many moods, who made you promise you wouldn't come tonight, explained it all from her folding chair. Deep, deep beneath the mechanical response to Mr. Tucker's urgings, a call was going out, an invitation to gather under the music to make common cause. Anticipation rippled the shingles on the bandstand, a yearning audible only to young hearts. They played for their friends, as you once did, a call to renew the face of this tired old earth. Age had taught you better, but they were still unprotected. Rigid as frozen reeds under Mr. Tucker's inflexible baton, inside they bubbled with plan and promise. Their song was heard by friend and classmate; behind faces taut with concentration, the hidden theme set young spirits to dancing.

Youth are the heralds of hope in any age. It is they who bring good news to a cynical society. You were with them once. You believed that cripples would walk and lepers would be cleansed. Even the deaf would hear the fanfare that sang in your soul. You would bring life to your languishing brothers and sisters. You would be another Christ, answering the Baptist's timid disciples with dynamic truth.

Can you remember the day the music stopped? For most of us, it didn't happen all at once. The sound died gradually; indeed, it took years for us to give in to the white noise of the adult world, that constant buzz of protective conversation which stifles the word of hope and dismisses as naive an exclamation of wonder. Many dreams came a cropper, many platitudes were imparted. Gradually you lost pitch, tone and voice to the sound track of tedium. One day you began to say things you didn't mean; what you meant, you dared not say. You finally fit in.

Is it naive to pray for naiveté, to ask the Lord to wipe away the film of pessimism grown thick in our winters of discontent? Some would say that all prayer must be for the possible; they point to a world which, despite endless petitions for reform and restoration, is still going to hell in a handbasket. Better to ask merely for the strength to survive, to step carefully around the stumbling blocks on a path that will never be anything but rocky. Salvation, redemption, serenity are dreams that will only come true hereafter. Here, hoping quickly gives way to coping.

Don't be too careful in your prayer. Don't restrict your petitions to the possible. God is not bound by our cramped horizons. Neither are his dreams for humankind limited to the familiar. Yes, God has dreams, plans for you and your world, hopes reflected in hopeful Christians who dare with Robert Kennedy to imagine things that never were and say, "Why not?" You and I and everyone on this planet are here because of God's transcendent vision. It was our vision once, as we burst into the world. Every newborn knows it, understands precisely why she or he has been sent out. Pity they cannot speak, but is it too much to suppose that an infant is inarticulate precisely because of the ineffability of the dream? Out of the mouths of babes comes gibberish to the world-weary, but to the Lord, enthusiasm and high praise.

When we look upon the optimism of the young only with concern for the day they hear the melancholy truth, we betray our lack of faith in the omnipotence of God. Who, if not God, whispers to a child of this straitened society that all things are possible? Who else could convince the gangling teenager that the Holocaust and Hiroshima were aberrations, that the agony of Beirut and the scourge of AIDS are not part of the plan? Only the divine Dreamer, who did not resign himself to that final cry from Golgotha, but fashioned from cosmic tragedy a new way of living. It was not finished; it was just beginning.

There must be a place for the child in our prayer. Gathering clouds of despair force us to an interior level of need deeper than nostalgia can plumb, back beyond our first conscious memories to a time when God's voice was clear and his power transparent. For each of us there was a hidden moment when the Creator said, "See, I make all things new!" That moment is the source of the prayer for naiveté. Because they need not stretch back so far to the primordial truth, our children live in hope. We can learn much from them, much about the spirituality of joyful anticipation. Our prayer is to recapture some of their resilience, to remember in an age stiff with pessimism the promise of a new creation.

Deep within,
a promise sung,
amazing grace poured out
upon the young.

Still the sound,
yet understood
by babes expecting naught
but endless good.

Warn them, LORD,
before the day
when life's discordant dirge
insures dismay.

129

Hold! Hear not
this cynic's plea;
of hope newborn, dear LORD,
oh, sing to me.
    Amen.

Winged Victory

[Jesus] said to [his] disciples: "Therefore I tell you, do
not worry about your life and what you will eat, or about
your body and what you will wear. For life is more than
food and the body more than clothing. Notice the rav-
ens: they do not sow or reap; they have neither store-
house nor barn, yet God feeds them. How much more
important are you than birds! Can any of you by worry-
ing add a moment to your lifespan? If even the smallest
things are beyond your control, why are you anxious
about the rest?" (Lk 12:22-26).

It fell with no rhyme to its descent, like a leaf in the warm
wind, like a bright yellow leaf tossed from a shivering poplar.
The smoke in its wake described a knotted helix, a crazy scrawl
for help against a cold, blue sky. Necks stretched upward stran-
gled the sound of the crowd. Only those who lowered their gaze
in fear of what they might see were able to draw a raspy breath.
The Stearman leveled out upside down just over the runway,
waggled its wings, did half a barrel, and landed on three points.
Only then, with their chins on the ground, did the onlookers release a sigh of relief; the daredevil bounded from the cockpit to
grateful applause from enthusiasts already craning their necks
for the next attempt to repeal the law of gravity.

All afternoon, above the stubble of clover and alfalfa
known as the municipal airport, fragile craft had rolled and
looped and dived as their pilots flouted the conventional wisdom
of the townspeople. Men were taking the most foolish chances, a
thousand times more foolish than investing in the stock market
or voting Democratic. These fliers were "risking certain
death," as the breathless announcer said again and again over
the PA. At first, you had been disappointed to find that the *Baron*

von Rand Air Devils consisted of only three grizzled pilots, their vintage biplanes, and an announcer. Where were last year's Mustangs and P-40's? Still, the staged dogfights aided mightily by the announcer's hyperbole produced a sky full of machines spewing smoke, maneuvering in lethal cannon fire, pitching over at the top of a victory roll . . . enough close-coupled action to make you hold your breath and clench your fists. More than once you turned to see if anyone suspected the depth of your involvement. None of your friends seemed to notice.

The finale was a full-power climb "to the edge of endurance of man and machine." Together, the three planes shot straight to the stratosphere. "Which will falter?" shouted the announcer. "Who will survive?" One by one, the planes fell over on their backs as they approached "the limits of the earth's attraction." You avoided asking yourself why such a substantial decrease in gravity would not permit the planes to break free. Instead, you drew in your breath as they fluttered to earth, eagles in a maelstrom, brave men fighting for control until the last possible moment required for a perfect landing. Safely down, the Jenny and the Spad rattled toward the hanger; the yellow Stearman rolled toward the crowd, toward the booth, toward the ticket seller. A nudge from your friend said your hour had come.

The year before, you chickened out after making the mistake of letting your buddies go up first. Their weak smiles brought no color to their ashen faces as they stumbled away from the World War II fighters. It was hard to swagger on shaky legs. Then, you thought better of holding up your end of the bargain; you swallowed your self-respect and kept your feet firmly on the ground. So, after months of ragging, you had to go up this time, and you knew you had to go first. Logic told you that ten minutes was just a tick of the clock, that these pilots didn't have a death wish, that an open cockpit was no more dangerous than a closed one, that the Stearman was tried and true, that. . . . The engine caught and roared and drowned out logic. The weathered furrows in the field made something unsavory come up in your throat even before the wheels spun free.

This Air Devil wasted no time when it came to helping young men prove their mettle. His initial climb punched you so far back in your seat that you quickly tightened your safety harness two more notches. You needn't have hurried this adjustment for the plane was a steady rocket straight up affording the pilot time enough to reach forward and check your belt and shake a warning finger. When he was satisfied that you were secure, he leveled off, put on his own harness for the first time, and sent the machine into an Immelmann turn so violent that you couldn't breathe. Then a triple roll, or rather two-and-a-half, and a half. Your comb fell out of your jacket, tipped your nose, and flew to the earth above your head. The last half of the roll wrenched you into what you thought was a blackout. Perhaps you had simply screwed your eyelids so tight that you saw blood. Then, two loops at the tops of which the plane actually stood still while you hung upside down again from your thin straps. Finally, a climb as steep as the first, culminating at the apex in a complete loss of control as the plane descended tail-first, engine coughing, spars and wires screaming. He had lost it. He had pushed past the limit. Through slit eyes, you saw the flaps slapping back and forth with the gyrations of the plane as it whirled, now nose-first, to the earth. You called on God; without guile or shame, you protested this fate, this foolish sacrifice of innocent life, this death on the altar of bravado.

The ground rushed up, the pilot cursed, a wire snapped, the plane leveled, floated, hit the ground hard, bounced and hit again. The bean field was behind the hangar, so your friends merely crossed the road to get to the plane, to point at the sprung landing gear, to turn up their noses at what covered the front of your jacket. The pilot still sat in the cockpit cursing the plane, banging on the stick. In the background, the voice of the announcer was subdued as he closed up shop and guaranteed a refund for each ticket to ride. "Getting too dark." You crouched among the beans and shivered. The breeze had gone suddenly cold against the falling sun.

That night in bed as you turned gingerly to find the position least painful to your stiff limbs and bruised ribs, the folly of pride lay with you. At first, you assured yourself that you had indeed triumphed over the elements, that you had survived the misjudgments of an over-the-hill pilot, that you had by sheer will brought a crippled machine back to earth. But the heartless moon of humiliation fitfully illuminated a semicircle of young men standing two steps away from an animal quivering on its haunches dressed in a stained flight jacket. That was the scene flashing on your ceiling. And the sound? The sound was truth, a scream from your cockpit when you knew the pilot had lost control. As the plane began to fall back on its tail, you had cried out to God to save you not from embarrassment but from "certain death." It had not been a plea for respect that settled like a dark mantle upon the tableau of reality in that bean field. It was the echo of a death rattle heard by only three: The pilgrim, who saw himself scattered on the earth; the guide, who cursed and fought for control; the Mercy, who saw pride go before a fall and leapt to save.

Our prayer reaches back over the decades as we remember with astonished gratitude the God who tolerated our youthful quests for acceptance. How many times did we justly merit our own demise? How many times did we, in our need to prove our worth, deliberately refuse to call upon the Name until it was too late? And how many times did he step abruptly from the mercy seat and give us back our lives?

Although it is not pleasant to recall, we force ourselves to picture the danger we wooed so long ago, to hear our callow voices defying the laws of nature and logic: the accelerator held

to the floorboard, the drunken challenge to fight, the swim beyond the reef, the whoop and holler of cat-and-mouse among the
moving boxcars. Too young to die? Even then, we knew someone who wasn't. We had shuffled through doorways draped in
black, mumbled to red-eyed parents slumped on the sofa, carried our mothers' covered dishes into the kitchen. It didn't last
long, that unfocused feeling of ineffectiveness and foreboding. A
night or two of waking dreams, of feeling the final pain she felt,
of using the common sense he apparently forgot . . . and then it
was over, replaced by a new season, a new challenge, a new plan
to prove ourselves.

Now we have better things to worry about, everyday pres-
sures youth cannot know. We see with wiser eyes God's saving
hand in more mundane difficulties. Perhaps, by his grace, we
have even reached that time in life when the once strident cry for
applause has been muted. Each prayer of the mature Christian
contains a word of gratitude for being allowed to see another
sunrise. Still, we must not let the habit of survival cause forgetfulness. In a more reckless day, we lived too much on the edge.
For the precipice that didn't crumble, for the leap restrained, we
are grateful. For the life we still possess in spite of our best efforts
to throw it away, we give thanks to a vigilant God. For the times
we called out too late, only to find it is never too late for his rescue, we acknowledge a merciful God. The fatal step was not
taken, the hand of fate was stayed: an ingrate was repaid with
understanding. Praise the Protector of children and fools.

A bill received,
a payment due;
no need to list each date and place
of heedless purchase, empty sale.
We pushed our luck,
outspent the rest;
the price of life concerned us not.
On borrowed time who keeps a tab?
But now the cost is mounting up,
ten thousand days with interest
until a little more than half
a life is owed. . .
the note is called?
So many times did you refuse
your profit, LORD, yet still we plead:
Extend our loan
just one more day.
                    Amen.

Nine the Hard Way

The woman saw that the tree was good for food, pleasing to the eyes, and desirable for gaining wisdom. So she took some of its fruit and ate it; and she also gave some to her husband, who was with her, and he ate it. Then the eyes of both of them were opened, and they realized that they were naked; so they sewed fig leaves together and made loincloths for themselves.

When they heard the sound of the LORD God moving about in the garden at the breezy time of the day, the man and his wife hid themselves from the LORD God among the trees of the garden. The LORD God then called to the man and asked him, "Where are you?" He answered, "I heard you in the garden; but I was afraid, because I was naked, so I hid myself." Then he asked, "Who told you that you were naked?" (Gn 3:6-11).

Little Norma felt like crying. In fact, she may well have been shedding a few tears, but she was so nervous she couldn't tell tears from perspiration. The shocking news had made the sweat pop out on her forehead. Paulie Stanton had been left at home. His mother had caught him at five o'clock that morning sitting at the kitchen table drinking a glass of milk. He had broken his midnight fast.

Paulie's dazzling white First Communion suit would stay in the closet that April morning. It would remain in its paper sheath for nearly two years until Mrs. Stanton, in a fit of long-delayed spring housecleaning, would remove it to find the yellow stain of age creeping down the back of the coat. She would put it in the attic for the Thanksgiving Clothing Drive. It may still be there; Paulie's mother was never very fastidious. She didn't worry about details like Norma's mom who had tied their refrigerator door closed with a jump rope the night before First Communion.

Her mother was giving thanks for all the disasters that didn't happen as she drove home after dropping Norma off at church for the final practice. Father was such a stickler for precision. That German blood always told. Right in front of the nuns he allowed as how a practice one hour before Mass would remedy any daydreaming the good sisters had permitted during a month of Friday afternoon drills. She thought back to the sisters who prepared her own second grade class for their First Communion and how Sister Cyprian would scare them silly with tales of little boys and girls who chewed their fingernails and broke their fast. She thought of the jump rope girdling the Frigidaire. That was Sister Cyprian's doing. Dan would have laughed. She saw again the way his nose crinkled. Her mind was far from the road. She didn't see the other car weaving from shoulder to shoulder.

Father reminded the boys and girls that they would march in two-by-two and sit next to their parents in reserved pews. Norma said a little prayer for her daddy, then thought of the plans she and her mother had made to have a quiet breakfast at home. She pictured Paulie's glass of milk, his white moustache and his round eyes when sleepy, rumpled Hilda Stanton barged into the kitchen.

After the practice, the sisters prodded them into the basement so parents could put the finishing touches on their suits and dresses. Norma got very worried when she couldn't find her mother. Sister Mary David—Merry Christmas, the kids called her because she was so jolly and round—took Norma's hand and tried to calm her fears. She walked beside her back upstairs to the vestibule telling her she was sure her mother would be in the pew. She wasn't. Norma marched in with the rest of the class and sat down in that long, yawning pew. It seemed to stretch across the whole church with the next family vanishing in the distance. Not until the Epistle when the congregation sat down did anyone notice the quietly weeping little girl with the empty places on either side of her. Although no other sound could be heard above Father's Prussian roar, her shoulders were obviously shaking. A man rose from the very last pew and tiptoed up the side aisle to Norma's row. He sat at her right just as Mrs. Stanton moved to her left side. She was sobbing too. Then a young man who had been standing by the back door came forward, then two maiden ladies from out of town. In all, nine new parents were sitting next to Norma when Father concluded the reading with his patented rolling ''r's.''

Norma's mother got out to inspect the damage. The reckless driver had forced her off the road and into the shallow ditch, then sped on. The sign she hit was sticking out of the grille, but the motor was still running, so she got in, bumped back onto the road, and drove home. She had only 20 minutes to do her hair. She dressed hurriedly and ran back to the car. It wouldn't start, wouldn't even turn over. The sign post had pierced the battery; all the power was in a sizzling puddle under the car. She tried calling some friends, but they had already left for Mass. Her only two neighbors at the end of this narrow country lane were gone too. She knew she couldn't make it.

She went into the back yard where Dan had spent so many hours toward the end, to the little grotto he had used his failing strength to build. There she knelt before the white plaster figure of the Sacred Heart and thought of the radiant dresses and suits at church so tiny along the big center aisle. Using the worn novena card her mother had given her, she prayed for her daughter, begged God to somehow make it right, to protect Norma from the awful sadness that was about to come down upon her. She knew she was rushing the prayers; the nine meditations were never meant to be said in one day. But this was an emergency. There, at the foot of the gleaming statue, she felt that it was alright, that he understood.

A very worried little girl was comforted as she stood before Father that day with nine new parents smiling behind her. Of course, the pastor's sense of order did not allow him to approve of such an odd scene, this large and disparate group of townsfolk and strangers, church-goers and now-and-thens. Neither did decorum permit the question, but if he had asked them why they had changed their seats, they would have said something quite prosaic: "The little girl was all alone," meaning that this celebration was about Communion and there was a little girl lacking communion. They had felt something, a murmur of the heart. Deep in that place where we listen for God's voice, they sensed the cadence of urgent repetition, the accents of maternal love. It wasn't a perfect prayer, but it was a confident prayer alive with the certainty that one little girl would not be deprived of union with God in the heart of Jesus. It was a mother's prayer this motley group knew in their hearts, a prayer so powerful that God's word must be formed around it. Even God cannot refuse a mother's prayer.

After Mass, Norma and her breathless, disheveled mother were reunited in the church basement. Father himself had whispered to an usher at the second collection to leave early. Mr. Bemis didn't spare the horses and found her still kneeling in front of the Sacred Heart. On the way back, he filled her in on "the darndest thing I ever did see in church." Unfortunately, he could name only two of the angels of mercy. After a tearful hug at the reception, Norma herself added but one more name, that of Hilda Stanton. She was certain, though, of the number: nine. "I had nine new mommies and daddies." Her mother touched the novena card in her pocket.

Nine men and women heard in their hearts God's word formed around the imperfect prayer of a worried mother. It was not her theological sophistication that moved them to their special ministry; it was the power that Jesus gave her plea as he transformed it into saving grace. They left their pews to stand beside a little girl in need. Her need was to know that she had not been abandoned by the world. They gave her human communion. Her need was also to know she had not been abandoned by

Jesus. He gave her Holy Communion. It all happened because a mother said nine prayers faster than she should have and tied a jump rope around the refrigerator.

Because the Eucharist is the most sublime of all prayers, we tend to think that worthy participation requires a matching nobility of motive and character. The universality of Christ's invitation, especially his compassionate appeal to sinners, belies this inaccurate supposition. The Eucharist is not a reward for perfection, but balm for the troubled soul. Each of us takes a separate path to Holy Communion. We limp forward, hobbled with infirmity or age. We stumble down the aisle blinded by regret for our sins. We step up and step back, hesitating over our lack of worth. Risking all, we take a deep breath and plunge ahead anyway, impelled by the deepest need for union with the source of healing and forgiveness. While we know we can never measure up, we know as well that we cannot live without this ultimate sign of our human dignity. Christ calls us to join our flesh and blood to his, to make a gift of ourselves, our strengths and our weaknesses, to be transformed by his love and made a fit offering for his Father. This call to Eucharistic union is heard in many voices and has many accents; it can be muffled by pride or superstition, hypocrisy or despair. Still, it sounds from the source, the font of affirmation with whom we long to be united.

When entering the prayer of the Eucharist, it may be wiser to forget your First Communion; the memory has been so overladen with the myth of purity that it can form a stumbling block. The mature Christian knows better than to mourn lost innocence. A second-grader's untainted conscience is a blessing of circumstance, not cultivation. To hesitate before the communion minister because one no longer has the pristine soul of an eight-year-old is to deny that the meaning of Christ's message is victory over sin and death.

Instead of lamenting the long exile from Eden, think of your most recent communion, the one last week. There you stood in your weakness, promising to clean up your act. In the seven days since, you fought the good fight against habits developed over months and years. If you made even an incremental improvement, proclaim your "Amen" in gratitude for receiving strength you alone could not muster. If you fell back, thank the Lord for accepting your sorrow and your promise of renewed openness to his power to save.

God still walks in the garden, still whispers to children in the breezy time of the day. But he is here among the brambles too, calling to us, competing with the raucous cries of carrion crows for our attention. "Come to the table I have set for you," he says. "Come with your dreams and disappointments to sit and sup with my Son. I send him as proof of your value."

How long it's been since you and I
    meandered down the garden path,
        in muted conversation dared
            to name the wonders that we shared.

        What think you of the stars, my child?
        What wags the puppy's tail, my LORD?
    Your stainless angels gently spread
white roses on the path ahead.

Yet I would trade, and have indeed,
    that unpicked paradise we knew
        to spend today beside your Son
            who walks among what choice has spun.

142

His word describes not joy decreed
but consecrates the jumbled now,
assuring us of liberty,
the essence of our dignity.

If all was lost, now all is gain
for children thrust from Eden's gate
who grow apace amid the strife;
the chosen choose your Christ, the life.
Amen.

The Vergers

When the days for his being taken up were fulfilled, he resolutely determined to journey to Jerusalem, and he sent messengers ahead of him. On the way they entered a Samaritan village to prepare for his reception there, but they would not welcome him because the destination was Jerusalem. When the disciples James and John saw this they asked, "LORD, do you want us to call down fire from heaven to consume them?" Jesus turned and rebuked them, and they journeyed to another village (Lk 9:51-56).

For years you were sure that Aunt Myrt and Uncle Ambrose were unique among all God's creatures. Not only did he throw away the mold when he finished with these two characters, he forgot where he dropped the blueprints, and very shortly thereafter he forgot Myrt and Ambrose. He set them spinning and turned his attention to other matters.

Did they spin! Knoxville, Butte, Tampa, Texas City. Never more than a year in any one place, then off to Cincinnati or Wichita or Memphis. Any place where folks needed electricity, Ambrose would put his welder's flame at their disposal. Myrt would follow to find the apartment and locate the dramatic society. Self-styled "children of the boards," they added well-traveled humor to any production. Once, in Little Rock, so you were told, they managed to turn "Death of a Salesman" into a comedy with Willy Loman modeling dresses. It was another uncle who whispered this to you; he had a Masters in English and taught honor students at East High. He didn't like Ambrose's red suspenders or Myrt's orange hair. He wasn't alone in his disapproval.

Your family, especially those on your father's side, stood

foursquare against the liberal aura Myrt and Ambrose brought to family gatherings and to the family reputation. First of all, they didn't have any children. Given the circumstances, that might have been just as well, but without kids you don't know what responsibility is. Worse, they never stayed in one place. Of course, neither did the need for rigging welders, but what kind of job is that anyway for a man with a college degree? Then this business about acting, putting on make-up, telling jokes over a microphone. It was too much for your mother's side too. Except to your mother herself and to her unreliable and unmarried sister, Ambrose's yellow convertible and Myrt's trousers said it all: not to be trusted, especially with children.

That's why you saw them only on holidays. Even when some new job opened up in the tri-state area, you were not taken to their latest apartment for one of the rare visits your father agreed to. "Better to go there and leave early," he sighed. And as for your mother asking her brother over, well, the boy would have to go to Aunt Ellen's. Your mother knew how that would look so she never invited Ambrose and Myrt. Thus, they became the mystery couple, the exotic, obviously disreputable black sheep who were allowed to mingle with polite society only when it was absolutely necessary, and only when they lived within a radius of one hundred miles. You probably saw them a total of six times before you graduated from high school. Since you judged them to be the life, the very soul, of each one of those rare reunions, you never accepted your elders' estimation of them.

At one Christmas party, they came dressed as Mr. and Mrs. Claus, but introduced themselves as Bertrand Russell and Gertrude Stein. Not everyone knew the claims to fame of these personages—you, a sophomore, certainly didn't—but most were fascinated by their 20-minute dialogue in front of the Christmas tree on the pros and cons of believing in Santa. Later, the English teacher grumped that no one else had a costume and that some of the ideas put forth were really quite vulgar. But you

noticed his rapt gaze. On a Fourth of July, they juggled spark-
lers, threw ladyfingers under the pinochle players' table, and
sang "It's a Grand Old Flag" accompanying themselves on ac-
cordion (Ambrose) and zither (Myrt). Every performance
ended with impressions of current celebrities. Myrt's forte was
her imitation of one star imitating another. To the chagrin of
those hanging on every word and gesture, neither ever identified
their targets. You assumed that was the mark of a true profes-
sional. It became a ritual for you to test your guesses after the
routine: Bette Davis doing Edward G. Robinson, Lionel Barry-
more doing Harry Truman. No one else went up to them or
spoke to them. Although you thought you pleased them with
your interest, they were quick to step away when your father
glowered from the doorway. Not to be trusted with children.

You were a sophomore again, this time at State, when you
got a call shortly after the spring break from Valerie, your vir-
ginal aunt. She was in hysterics, something about being jilted
and would you help her get even. Why was she calling you all the
way from home? What could you do anyway? She said you could
at least come over to dinner. It was Myrt doing Aunt Val to a
"t." They had just moved to the Capital for a job. You accepted
with a grateful laugh; you hadn't seen them for nearly two years.
And you weren't a child any longer so you could trust them.

It came as no surprise that the walls were covered with
posters and playbills tracing their lives in the glow of the foot-
lights. The movers were due tomorrow, but the treasures of the
theater always traveled with the couple in the trunk of their car.
Myrt told you between rave reviews that sometimes it took two
weeks for the furniture to catch up. The walls couldn't stay bare
for that long, especially when new-found children of the boards
made get-acquainted visits. "We'll eat on this card table as long
as we have to," here Ambrose's voice deepened dramatically,
"but we can't live without the *life*."

Both had been quite animated when you first arrived at the
apartment. Pride in their life in the theater bubbled over as they

147

recalled different plays and roles. At dinner, however, the subject turned to family. Myrt admitted that you were the first of all their nephews and nieces who had ever come to visit any of their "roosts." She wondered if you or the others knew why you had never been allowed to come to see them. At first, you hesitated. But, after all, you were a college man, you were an adult visiting other adults, and you were not going to tell them anything they didn't already know. As if to prove this, Ambrose beat you to the punch. "We move around, we act in plays, and we don't have any children. Right?" "Reet," said Joe College. "Wrong," said Myrt. "It's because we didn't get married in church."

It turned out that Myrt had been married before, twice, in fact, when Ambrose went to your grandfather. There was a "doozy" of an argument. It was either Myrt or the family. The family lost. The old man forbade anyone to accompany them to the judge's chambers. Your mother and Aunt Val went, and they were nearly kicked out of the house for their trouble. Myrt and Ambrose began their wanderings. They weren't invited to a family gathering until three years after Grandpa died. By that time, they were too different, and it was obvious that God was punishing them by withholding children. The acting? Well, Ambrose said that he suspected it started as a way of coping with a world that shunned them. They could be acceptable in costume, whether it was on a stage or at a summer resort or in a living room on Thanksgiving Day. It was the only life for them.

At that point, Myrt signaled the end of Psychology 101 by going into her Ed Wynn routine. That was fine with you; too many family secrets at one sitting made you feel like a snoop. For the next hour you laughed until your sides ached at the two mimicking your aunts and uncles, even your father. You left with a promise to come back often, but you knew you would have to think about that later. After all, Uncle Ambrose and Aunt Myrt were "living in sin," as she put it. So then how could they be so cheerful and carefree, so . . . good? You had some thinking to do.

In Luke's gospel, the Samaritans rejected Jesus' messengers because of clannish enmity; we too can fancy ourselves as righteous keepers of the flame. We turn our backs on those who take a different path to the kingdom. Often these limping pilgrims have much to teach. Unlike James and John, Myrt and Ambrose did not call down fire upon their fastidious family. They accepted the long rehabilitation mandated by their unbending relatives. In the process, they became the entertainers, oddballs, good for a laugh, but keep the kids away. During your subsequent visits you learned how they resigned themselves to seek no more than an annual entry into the halls of orthodoxy. "It took a while," Ambrose confided to you once when Myrt was out doing her one-woman show in a shopping mall. "It took nearly 10 years of licking our wounds, but we finally said to each other, 'Thank God, it's only once a year.'" They still go back if they're within the radius. They still entertain. But now they understand their role as that of cheering up a rather cheerless breed. As Myrt said once in her best Tallulah Bankhead growl: "You know, dahling, if God was as mean as your family thinks, Ambrose and I would still be living in your home town."

Remember them to God—the gadflies, the rapscallions, the characters who run full tilt against respectability. Be not, however, condescending in your prayers, for these Don Quixotes are sent into our world by their Protector. Yes, he sends them, commissions them to prick the bubble of pretension in which too many of the righteous seal themselves. Their ministry is that of provocation, their reward the tiniest spark of self-realization in a hidebound heart. They sense the outlandish in each of us—the odd habit, the bizarre daydream, the embarrassing eccentricity—and hold it to the light, not so much for ridicule as for recognition. Our reaction is understandable but subtly graced by the messengers' divine patron. Harrumphing conventionality is just another way of covering our eyes with our hands. Still, we do peer through fingers shaking from a muffled laugh at ourselves as we really are.

Name them before God, the teasing truthtellers in your life. Recall the lonely faces on the periphery. They spin into our fixed orbits like shooting stars, then out again into darkness to let the wounds heal, theirs and ours. Granted, no matter how necessary the medicine, it is hard to be grateful to the physician at the moment when needle meets quivering flesh. The scribes and Pharisees were not at all pleased by the ministrations of the country doctor from Galilee, but a race and a world needed a shot of truth serum. Today, when you need a booster, remember the jesters stand with Jesus.

With the self-satisfied of every age, we vent our frustrations upon square pegs in round holes; with those struggling for the wisdom which comes only from honest self-appraisal, we should welcome these prophets in motley. Naturally, our prayer is hesitant, given the fragility of our defenses. Yet, our prayer is also trusting, given the healing power of a compassionate God. Our prayer is: "Send in the clowns."

The thorn in an Apostle's side,
　the lawsuits never won,
　　the lisp which caused a duke to frown
　　　upon his bumptious son,
　　　　the voices of a peasant girl,
　　　　　the bugler's shadowed birth,
　　　　　　the hate that forced a chosen race
　　　　　　to roam the hostile earth.

The vexing grain within the shell
  begets such pearls as these:
    Hail, Paul of Tarsus, Honest Abe,
    and Winnie with his "V's";
        brave Joan of Arc stands out in front
        with Satchmo blowing "Charge,"
        while from a lowly remnant springs
        the saving Word writ large.

        O LORD, when I fall back undone
        by struggles with my lot,
            remind me of those victors whom
            adversity begot.

        Amen.

Dirt-Daubers

I consider that the sufferings of this present time are as nothing compared with the glory to be revealed for us. For creation awaits with eager expectation the revelation of the children of God; for creation was made subject to futility, not of its own accord but because of the one who subjected it, in hope that creation itself would be set free from slavery to corruption and share in the glorious freedom of the children of God. We know that all creation is groaning in labor pains even until now; and not only that, but we ourselves, who have the firstfruits of the Spirit, we also groan within ourselves as we wait for adoption, the redemption of our bodies. For in hope we were saved. Now hope that sees for itself is not hope. For who hopes for what one sees? But if we hope for what we do not see, we wait with endurance (Rom 8:18-25).

Everybody called them "dirt-daubers," those people who lived in basements without the benefit of a house on top. Their cement block homes sunk ten feet into the cold land looked from the surrounding hills like dozens of trap doors giving access to the bowels of the earth. A closer inspection revealed three feet of wall above the ground providing the base for a flat roof of tar paper. At one corner stood a man-sized covered entry like a solitary guardhouse protecting the first steps of the enclosed stairwell. The stairs led down to the basement of what the dirt-daubers hoped would someday be that single family dwelling they had dreamed of all through the war.

At first, you joked with the boys at work about it. You had never been in a bomb shelter during the war, but when peace broke out, you moved into one. Then, it was funny, but after two and a half years of this stifling existence, you felt like a mole. Would your eyes be able to take the sun tomorrow? Were the kids digging through the wall in their room? Would they get away and join the others in the maze of tunnels beneath the city?

The thoughts of a fevered mind, of course, but you had a right to be feverish. What was wrong with the system? You didn't know if it was government agencies or the lumber companies or the planing mills that were holding back the wood. You only knew that you and Karen and the kids were not going to end up like the Eppmans who, after waiting over four years for their material, sold it the day it was delivered and instead bought more cement blocks to expand their basement. The pale Artie and Esther and their sallow children had grown so accustomed to living underground that they were afraid to live above.

Sometimes, though, a glimmer of what the Eppmans saw lit up your inverted castle. It could be, after all, very cozy, especially in the living room where you had paneled the walls with the oak borrowed from your brother-in-law's rumpus room. As a 4-F, Nat had stayed home and made connections. Being a man of some sensibility, he politely waited until the war ended to build. Three years later, he was doubling the size of his palace on Burton Hill. All he wanted was the wood returned for his new den above the garage. So your living room came close to deserving its name, at least until 10:00 p.m. when it became your bedroom. In came the rollaway, out flew contented thoughts. The sump pump whirred, the furnace roared. You stared at the ceiling, the floor of the house that never was, and wondered if Artie and Esther dug tunnels at night. Maybe they were just outside that cold wall, listening to the two of you curse your fate while they rubbed their whiskers with their paws.

There came a time when the plans were never taken from their honored place under the silverware case. You both knew them by heart down to the square footage of a bathroom and the width of a closet door. A friend of Nat did them for you, an architectural school drop-out who was struggling to make it as a

builder in a world without wood. Someday things would loosen
up and he would have his name and business number on plans
stashed in basements all over the county. He was no piker when it
came to drawing on your credit line. For you, a grand chalet, two
and a half stories in Elizabethan crossbeams and wainscotting.
You hadn't realized it was your dream home until he unrolled it
on your damp floor early in your first subterranean spring. He
had managed to pull your most impalpable fantasies into corners
and windows and dormers. The wife's complaint about minimal
closet space triggered a flurry of erasing and the necessary modifications. Now you had something specific to hang a dream on.

In those early days, the muted tinkle of silver spoons and
forks was heard every evening as you pored over the plans. At
night, you dreamed not of the Eppmans' mud-flecked hides but of
actually walking from room to room and doing those things for
which the room was designed. In the foyer, you would hang up
your coat; in the bathroom, you would gargle and spit. Karen
said she had the same dreams. These hope-filled transports even
produced a name for the manse—Dreamland—that would be on
the sign next to the driveway. In that buoyant time, the darker
meaning escaped you both.

As the months piled up to crush your hopes, you became
more guarded, disturbing the silver less frequently. Neither of
you wanted to chance the loss of a closet here, a room there, perhaps a whole story. After two years, partial allotments of building
materials were being offered at exorbitant prices; there came the
recurring temptation to scale down the plans, to settle for a cot-
tage in order to get above ground. But you both steeled yourselves
and made a pact not to talk about the house, not to lure each other
into compromise. Finally, you each came to the end of your endurance at about the same time. Thirty-four months were awfully
close to three years, and look at the Eppmans. That last spring,
you both knew something was going to happen, something had to
give. After Easter, you began to talk seriously of renting an apartment in town and selling your plot, your realm, your Dreamland.

When the whistling through the tops of the propane bottles became shrill enough to wake you, you weren't surprised at the sudden storm. The evening before had been unusually muggy for April. Wrestling with the leaking rear tire in the oppressive humidity took so much out of you that you had given up without mounting the spare. There was such terrible static on the ten o'clock news that Karen turned it off before the weather. What did surprise you in the black dawn was the pitch of the wind, more piercing than you had ever heard it, a cat being tortured to death. When the scream was abruptly cut off, you knew the bottles were gone, flying missles at 125 pounds each. The night light dimmed once and died; the grinding of the clock on the sideboard stopped; the kids ran for your bed just as the covered entry shrieked and gave itself to a callous hand.

The paper said later that it took the tornado only 90 seconds to traverse the city's outskirts. It came with little rain; what you had thought was a deluge turned out to be thousands of pieces of shredded wood from the houses on Burton Hill. It was this rain of oak and pine rapping on your tar paper that kept you and the family huddled under the bed until the gray light fell through the high windows. The door at the bottom of the stairs was jammed. As you went for the crowbar, you saw the clock stopped at 4:25.

In your boyhood, you had always experienced a thrill of pride to hear your town described as situated "on the edge of Tornado Alley." The thrill was gone the day you pushed up through the debris-filled stairwell to where the covered entry had been. In the driveway, the jack still stood upright, but it supported no car. You thought you saw the old De Soto upside down at the end of the street. It was hard to tell, though, since everything was covered by a blanket of torn wood. Up on Burton Hill were the shells of the homes that had provided the blizzard. You saw your brother-in-law's great house still standing, but roofless.

Down your street, others were emerging from their basements, pointing to the devastation all around them. The path of destruction marched right down Burton Hill and stopped. The twister had continued, of course, but with the exception of some cars and covered entries and a bomb load of propane bottles, your street escaped. Maybe not escaped as much as survived. The storm had slapped your neighborhood but couldn't find enough to get a grip on. A special Tornado Edition of the paper two weeks later gave the final statistics: five killed, 137 injured, 39 homes destroyed, 104 badly damaged. By then, you had rebuilt your entry, installed new propane bottles, and were prowling the used car lots for something to match your jack.

Each of us has to learn that patience involves more than mere waiting. Patience is learning God's schedule and conforming our own to it. The tempo of worldly life demands gratification on demand. The tempo of life in God requires a rhythm of prayer and meditation as a background to discernment. In this patient rhythm, we pause to listen as God explains our real needs and describes his loving mercy. Those who are impatient never take the time to hear the word of blessing, never pause to measure what they want against what they need.

When you were a dirt-dauber, you found that what you hoped for and worked for and yearned for would have ended in kindling had God not taught you patience. In the endless delays and disappointments, you learned the loving rhythm of a God who shared your dream of hearth and home, but who in his mercy put your survival first. You have enjoyed a beautiful home for these many years now because you spent a muggy April night in the basement of a house that wasn't. The Master Builder had decided to wait.

There is something a bit incongruous about praying for patience. Meaningful prayer is itself an exercise in patience, a measured surrender to God's timetable. When appealing for the virtue required to put up with the frustrations of the job or the obstinacy of the children, we are tempted to expect little patience pills: Take one before each bruising encounter. Our aim, rather, should be to extend the attitude of prayer to those situations. In prayer, we have learned to wait, to count to ten, sometimes to count to a million. Prayer is an act of relinquishing our right to shake the world by its shoulders in favor of the working of God's more leisurely, more gentle grace. Practitioners of authentic prayer will want to apply what they've gained from their intimacy with God to their relationships with their fellow men and women.

The first thing God teaches us in prayer is that he has his own agenda. So accept the fact that your inert teenager or frenetic benchmate is living a life in a different cycle than yours. This doesn't mean you have to adopt a schedule to match, simply that you have to make adjustments. Since patience in prayer pleases God, your attempts at understanding the people in your life please them and increase the chances for a more pleasant concourse. Then there is the matter of dignity. In prayer, you glorify God in all his noble intentions; in patient relationships with others, you respond to their worth, giving them room to act positively rather than always reacting negatively to your pressing priorities. In all this, however, there is one important caveat. While using the characteristics of authentic prayer to enhance your associations with others, beware of confusing them with the Lord of Heaven and Earth, or their purposes with his plan. The motorist who jumps the light, the snide counter girl are not necessarily on the side of the angels. Patience does not mean approval of questionable intentions. The analogy of bringing the patience learned in prayer to the marketplace stops well short of praising perversity.

Remember, patience is more than waiting. In prayer, we lift up a world "groaning in labor pains even until now." Patient endurance does not preclude the petition that God might make haste to save. Nor does patient endurance of the foibles of our friends prevent us from offering a word to the unwise. A glory waits to be revealed; as Christians we are commissioned to assist that revelation.

Prickly, the itch
to show the way,
grasp loose strings,
quickly tie up the day.
Our balm is but to have
our say.

Patience, O LORD
is your design:
rope enough
not to hang but entwine
our frayed and frazzled lives
with Thine.
     Amen.

The School of Hard Knocks

He who spoils his son will have wounds to bandage,
    and will quake inwardly at every outcry.
A colt untamed turns out stubborn;
    a son left to himself grows up unruly.
Pamper your child and he will be a terror for you,
    indulge him and he will bring you grief.
Share not in his frivolity
    lest you share in his sorrow,
      when finally your teeth are
        clenched in remorse.
Give him not his own way in his youth,
    and close not your eyes to his follies (Sir
      30:7-11).

It wasn't resentment that you felt. He could have been a drinker or a skirt-chaser. The truth was that many of the wives on the block envied you, or so they said. Ruby complained all the time about how many evenings Pete spent at the bowling alley. And Tim Schlaumburg's fishing drove Betty up a tree. He was always after her about selling out and buying a houseboat. And poor Helen with Vinnie at the race track every day. They said you should count your blessings, having a man around the house and good with his hands to boot.

There it was. It was resentment after all, not so much of him but of what he put you through as you dodged the creations that poured forth from his workshop. Especially now that you were finally, really pregnant, the workshop became a cornucopia of credenzas, chairs, bookcases, tables, more than enough pieces to furnish the entire second floor of the house. How proud you had been when you got married. You had bragged to your friends that you wouldn't have to buy a stick of furniture. You would use your grandmother's things until they could be replaced with his handmade treasures, furniture that would outshine even the beautiful pieces he had made for his parents.

Replace them, he did. What with the overtime at the factory and your miscarriages, the pace had been slow at first. Weekends mostly were all he could squeeze in between nursing you and keeping Amalgamated's paperwork flowing. If love made the heart beat faster, his heart must have been going a mile-a-minute in the workshop. You used to watch, which didn't bother him at all. He was oblivious to your presence and to your childish jealousy as he caressed the supple mahogany and handled the cheap pine roughly. Jealousy soon turned to boredom; you returned to the kitchen to listen to your radio programs. The light in the workshop burned late on Saturdays and Sundays. You felt very safe, very married when you looked out the back window to see him sweating over the back-and-forth of a plane. You knew plenty of girls in the neighborhood who would be listening to *Suspense* alone.

It was the furniture itself. While he was filling the bedrooms and the upstairs hall, the secret was secure. It took over two years to replace all of Grandma's things up there and put them in storage for your sister when she got married. But with work slowing up at the plant and you big as a house, he had a lot more time. Although you never told him so, you once had a dream of him as Superman—by day, a lowly accountant keeping the pencils sharpened at Amalgamated; by night, the accomplished craftsman turning out handsome furniture with an easy stroke of the hammer and a quick twist of the screwdriver. You never told him of that dream for fear he would stay up all night and double his output, thereby doubling your resentment. No, the problem was not the time he spent in the workshop. The problem was not the number of pieces he made. The problem was the way they looked.

Your husband was not a craftsman. He wasn't a woodworker. He wasn't even a carpenter. When it came to building furniture, your husband was a sculptor. He hacked, he mauled, he split lumber until sometimes you thought you heard the forest scream. Most pieces looked as if he had started with a solid block of wood, then chipped away until its form approximated that of real furniture. He didn't know the meaning of counter-sinking. You incurred fresh scratches every week from protruding screws and nails on your headboard. There were dresser drawers that you had never been able to open. You thanked God for the four bureaus in your bedroom; together they featured five working drawers. Finish? Like a painter in *gouache,* he slapped on coat after coat of varnish and stain, alternating the layers until the grain was well masked and your skin stuck to every surface. All the while, he hummed in the workshop, turning out some new monstrosity, happy to be pleasing you, caring nothing that your compliments had stopped with his third project, the grotesque maple chandelier in the hall. He knew he was good.

Your resentment turned to dread when it became apparent even to him that the upstairs was becoming overpopulated. One day he finished the last of the 12 matching three-legged stools for the nursery. You held your tongue and didn't ask if he thought you were carrying a cow. The next Saturday, he worked all night to finish the first downstairs piece, a cedar umbrella stand. Now the girls would begin to see their error as they came to visit. Good with his hands, indeed. The first big piece would be a dining room table. You saw Helen and Ruby with their arms stuck to it, unable to rise, unable to flee its ominous bulk. And matching chairs, of course, with protruding screws to snag their nylons. On the next visit, they would gasp at the great Victorian coat rack into which he would set a mirror the size of the living room window. Would it be cracked? Just at one corner. Then, new kitchen cabinets with a convenient peg for the crowbar needed to open the drawers.

Your pregnancy gave you a new resolve. After all, your little girl would open her eyes in this house. What bizarre path would her fragile mind take as she stared at all those stools? You called his mother and told her you were coming over for a talk right away.

The next night, knowing he was itching to get out to the workshop, you pulled him back to his chair at Grandma's quite reasonable kitchen table. You had considered skirting the issue of quality and concentrating instead on quantity, but his mother's revelations persuaded you that this was the time for the whole truth.

He took it hard. The most difficult part was getting him to admit that his father, a journeyman carpenter, had to do a "little touching up" on each piece of furniture he built for his parents' house; he insisted the modifications were minor. Both parents always praised his work to high heaven. His eyes filled up when you told him of his mother's confession: "He wanted so to please, so we helped him a bit." As you softened still more her delicate yet devastating appraisals of his creations, you could sense him mentally going over each table and chair in their house, shuddering at the point where his work had ended and his father's began. Finally, there was a very long silence. His watery gaze rested on the rough and blotchy umbrella stand. He got up and carried it out to the workshop, pulling it apart with his bare hands.

There are many evils in the world against which parents should guard their children. There are many dangers that could prove fatal to a child without the protection of his or her elders. Common failure does not fall into these categories. In most cases, it is neither morally evil nor life-threatening. In truth, a youth who is protected from making mistakes learns little about life; parents who shield sons and daughters from the consequences of failure set them up for a mighty fall.

Your mother-in-law told you how much they both wanted their boy to follow in his father's footsteps. Even when it became painfully obvious that this sensitive teenager was all thumbs in the woodshop, his father made things right and praised him for work he had not done. Although he broke their hearts in choosing numbers over nails, they let the charade go on. The inevitable result was cold truth at a kitchen table.

Someone is failing at this moment, not in China or Tanzania, but right in your family circle. Even now, a young person is seeing a small dream shattered, a plan going awry. Against the weight of human events, they don't even move the scale—this bad mark on a test, that dropped ball, those little collapses of confidence in personal relationships or moral rectitude. But these setbacks are important to the one involved who is important to you, important enough to hold up to the Lord for his compassion.

Our prayer is not that God grant protection from failure, but that those we love might learn from their mistakes. This is especially true of our children who must come to see that the process of recognition, admission and remedy has no place for resignation. We ask that the reverses suffered may not be linked in the minds of the young to what is essential in them, a dignity, a value never diminished by coming in second or coming in last. We speak to One regarded during his public life as an egregious loser. To most of his contemporaries, the crucifixion of Jesus seemed to be the fitting climax to a ministry that assailed religious authorities, enraged his fellow townspeople, and disappointed his closest followers. It was a long time before the symbol of the cross became anything more than a reminder of a colossal fiasco.

To Christ, we commend the stumbling among us, asking that he lead them through the dark valley. He knows the way, he knows the strength required to endure; above all, he knows the brightness of a new day, a Sunday morning born of many dark Friday afternoons. Our petition is not that those dear to us be carried from glory to glory, but that young pilgrims on a road that will always be rocky may learn to pick themselves up, dust themselves off, and start all over again.

That resurrection Sunday,
 voices strained to tell the story:
He has triumphed over darkness,
 leading all to final glory.

That catastrophic Friday,
 Zion rang with lamentations:
He has lost the final struggle;
 gone, the futile hope of nations.

Of which the greater moment:
 brave example, wondrous rising?
LORD, you proved both miracles and
 fortitude are gifts worth prizing.
  Amen.

Earth Mother

The bows of the mighty are broken,
    while the tottering gird on strength.
The well-fed hire themselves out for bread,
    while the hungry batten on spoil.
The barren wife bears seven sons,
    while the mother of many languishes.
The LORD puts to death and gives life;
    he casts down to the nether world;
    he raises up again.
The LORD makes poor and makes rich,
    he humbles, he also exalts.
He raises the needy from the dust;
    from the ash heap he lifts up the poor,
To seat them with nobles
    and make a glorious throne their heritage
    (1 Sam 2:4-8).

On a Sunday in May the church relaxed. The stern visage of the Just Judge was replaced by the compassionate smile of the Virgin. Instead of the taut musculature of the Crucified straining upward, a fuller form caught the eye, directed it down to the folds of a blue robe draping the rough earth. The doctrinaire black and white of creed and stricture gave way to softly rustling waves of multicolored petals. May Crowning was about the colors of the church, about the delicate shadings from one flower to the next that revealed the vibrancy lying undiscovered all the year. This day, no rose was merely red, but crimson and vermillion and scarlet. No violet was blue, but aquamarine and azure and cerulean. The Mystical Body, that clear, crystal structure of sharp-edged saints, turned out to be a house of tints and shadows, a greenhouse with panes no longer forbiddingly brilliant, but translucent and welcoming, bidding you to come forward and see the riot of tones and values, the colors of life close to the earth.

May Crowning was about the music of means rather than ends. The sound that filled the house of God was different this day. The voices were still pure but now sprung from the honest loam rather than filtered through an ethereal veil. While tenors and sopranos remained aware that "the eye made blind by sin Thy glory may not see," they permitted themselves to be gently overwhelmed by altos and basses urging all to "bring flow'rs of the fairest, bring flow'rs of the rarest, from garden and woodland and hillside and vale." The music of the land, the scent of its delicate produce, the vivid hues of life drawn from the soil combined to remind the pale Christian that monitum and rescript cannot contain the fertile hopes, the rich promise upon which the church is built. Terrazzo will craze, hardwood will swell, and through the cracks will slip the teeming colors of sensate love, the pungent smell of sweating dancers, the harmony of gentle laughter. Into the church crept the earth of which its people were born. Into the people crept the freedom to celebrate their roots. On those May days so long ago, commoners turned to a Queen and saw their Mother. They lauded a Virgin with fleshly Child. They looked up to heaven and beheld a world in bloom.

Despite the Lady's lofty pedestal, she was a woman with her feet on the ground. Although the innocents in her court surrounded her in a cloud of white taffeta and twill, the essence of the earth could not be captured by a band of angels. She meant to stand among the people and, in spite of their best efforts, would not allow herself to be divinized. Who were they to lead her to a throne among the stars? She knew the veiny clay on which she stood.

Long ago she had sojourned in an unholy land and seen the rooted fruit of God's love plucked from the dry soil. So rare was a flower in that unfriendly clime that her sisters and brothers refused to believe it was real. It must be a ruse or some shallow growth, a changeling weed assuming for a moment the guise of ancient manna. They tore it out roughly and flung it down on the top of a hill outside the wall. She had seen this callous harvest, had heard the derisive laughter as petal and stem and root returned to the earth from which he was made, from which she was made, from which they were made. She meant to stand on this earth.

She accepted the title of Queen only to forestall that of Goddess. She consented to a crown, but not of sapphire and gold. It must be, rather, a tiara woven of hollyhocks and violets, petunias and pea blossoms, a very fragile crown that would wilt and fail in the heat of life. She lowered her head to the thrice-scrubbed hands of a sinless child, the unblemished representative of a sullied race. The intricate weave of vine and bud rested easily on her brow; its scent mingled with the essence of this commonplace people, with the colors and voices of her kin, those descendants of the reckless harvesters who uprooted the desert flower and threw him aside. The sentimental hymn swelled: Mothers dabbed at their eyes, fathers gulped. The little girl in the veil tottered for a moment on the high stool, then steadied herself by embracing the statue, her chubby arms encircling the plaster waist. Awakened to his duty by a chorus of gasps from the congregation, her freckled escort assisted her descent and delivered her safely to the front row.

It was done. A life of perfect humility ended with a coronation. At the bidding of her earthbound family, a powerless virgin was elevated to the side of God. Indeed, she sometimes seemed then to have power over him, to be able to change God's mind and stay his hand, to possess divine omniscience allowing her to "aid us ere our feet astray wander from Thy guiding way."

Suddenly, the pendulum swung. Today we are not even sure of the competence of God himself in matters such as relief from terrorism or protection from nuclear annihilation. Then, many of the sweet Marian hymns we sung contained no mention of her Son. Now, we are to be saved Christologically or not at all. And Christ turns out to be Jesus, who turns out to be a human being as well as God. No wonder the faithful are confused. It was all so clear then.

Rather than bemoan the sad state of belief in our day, we draw out of the crucible of change that which has been purified concerning the veneration of the Blessed Virgin. It is quite enough to know that she was a woman, not a goddess; a mother, not a surrogate; a spirit enfleshed, not an automaton; a sister drawn from the earth into a world of confusion; a contender in the arena called life. Out of the chaos of our time, we look to her to intercede on the side of peace. She knows how precious is a heart serene. She knows how dear is the price of brotherhood. She knows how delicate is the balance of discernment. She is one with the people she stands among on that May day when all of nature is in harmony. She draws into her heart of flesh the sounds and colors and smells of the earth on which she sets her foot. The Virgin Mother inclines her head. We may crown her, but not with precious jewels. Instead, we plait a circlet of common themes, of hopes and dreams for simple things like peace and faith and courtesy. She will wear this crown, knowing it will fade with our resolution, until the next time we send an innocent to place upon her gracious brow our pleadings and our promises.

The *Dogmatic Constitution on the Church* called the Blessed Virgin ''a sign of sure hope and solace for the pilgrim People of God'' (*Lumen Gentium,* 68). As the new Israel, we look to Mary to see the perfect flowering of an ancient race, the purest conception of our spiritual forebears who endured the long night with only hope to light their way. In her, the promise was fulfilled; to her, we offer prayers of hope that the promise may be fulfilled in us, that the Prince of Peace may be born anew in our land and in our hearts.

Because of our preoccupation with self, even God is thwarted in his desire to bless the wide earth with tranquillity. Pettiness and pride fill those places in the heart reserved for peace. In our frustration, we lash out at one another, scorpions in a basket, unable to escape injury, unable to keep from injuring even those we love. Again we turn to Mary, this time for solace amid the havoc we have wrought. Through her Son, she brings the comfort of a mother bending over her reckless children. Since she herself walked upon unfriendly soil, she knows our needs and calls forth the healing touch of her beloved Jesus. Our wounds are bound up, our frustrations are salved through the intercession of a mother who was and still is a woman of the earth.

We pray with the Fathers of Vatican Council II. ''Let the entire body of the faithful pour forth persevering prayer to the Mother of God and Mother of men. Let them implore that she who aided the beginnings of the Church by her prayers may now, exalted as she is in heaven above all the saints and angels, intercede with her Son in the fellowship of all the saints. May she do so until all the peoples of the human family, whether they are honored with the name of Christian or whether they still do not know their Savior, are happily gathered together in peace and harmony. . . '' (*Lumen Gentium*, 69).

O Mary, conceived without sin,
    pray for us
        in whom right and wrong endlessly contend.
O Mary, assumed into heaven,
    pray for us
        enchained by earthly ambition.

171

O Mary, Mother of the Savior,
    pray for us
        who seek salvation in the world.
O Mary, Queen of peace,
    pray for us
        who rend the fabric of mutual respect.
O Mary, Virgin pure and mild,
    pray for us
        who enthrone sensuality and call it love.
O Mary, faithful wife of Joseph,
    pray for us
        who bend our plighted vows.
O Mary, daughter of Israel,
    pray for us
        in whom the weed of prejudice takes root.
O Mary, handmaid of the LORD,
    pray for us
        who must do it our way or not at all.
O Mary, sister of the lowly,
    pray for us
        who value place above compassion.
O Mary, suffused in grace,
    pray for us
        who close our hearts to glory.
        Amen.

The Chosen

Three times I begged the LORD about this, that it might leave me, but he said to me, "My grace is sufficient for you, for power is made perfect in weakness." I will rather boast most gladly of my weaknesses, in order that the power of Christ may dwell with me. Therefore, I am content with weaknesses, insults, hardships, persecutions, and constraints, for the sake of Christ; for when I am weak, then am I strong (2 Cor 12:8-10).

It looked like a boiler complete with rivets all around holding the curved plates in place. It sounded like a boiler. Sixty times a minute a burst of air spurted from its porous piping causing it to jump and shudder with each exhalation. There the resemblance ended. Boilers constrained the explosive pressure of steam. This machine was powered from the outside; it wheezed and danced to the tune of a spasmodic compressor slung beneath its gray belly. Boilers didn't have windows to reveal the lightning and thunder of the forces contending within. This marriage of medicine and mechanics had four portholes set into its sides which laid bare the pale, powerless cast of wasting flesh.

You and Slomo went all the way back to kindergarten. His name was Richard—Ricky, as a child—until ninth grade when Coach picked him to start at center. Growing rapidly to 6'5", he was so gangly that he had to think about walking, had to concentrate on the movements of his legs lest he get tangled up and fall. This deliberate motion earned him the nickname, Slow Motion, and then, Slomo. So, no one was surprised on that February day in your senior year to read in the sports section: "Slomo Chosen All-State."

The following September, you packed your bags and

moved to a freshman dorm at State. Slomo's mother packed his bags, and his three gigantic uncles moved him to the Sister Kenny Institute. The D.A.R. had given you a partial scholarship for your essay and oration on Americanism; nobody knew who gave Slomo polio. Both the pools and the beach had been closed for two summers; his parents, like yours, didn't let him go to the movies after April; there had been no cases in your school for three years. He could hardly speak the first few times you visited him; he couldn't tell you how he got it or what it was like to be paralyzed. Back at the dorm, you imagined as you slipped under the covers that you were getting into an iron lung. It made you want to pray, but you felt guilty thanking God that you didn't get it when your best friend did.

Friendships are hard to maintain when one friend worries about tears when visiting another. You went every week at the beginning; since the hospital was just across town you had no excuse not to. Your urge to weep stopped when he regained his voice and all the bitterness began pouring out: "This is what I get for going to church every Sunday." He mentioned basketball only once during that first autumn, recalling a columnist who had compared him to the young George Mikan; he ended with a mean laugh at the joke God had played on him. He didn't listen to the games and wished that guy with the radio at the end of the ward would hurry up and die. You were secretly glad when they moved him back home to a specially equipped room off his mother's kitchen. You weren't doing him any good and he was getting you down.

It was impossible to lose track of a buddy in an iron lung, but you came close to it. By the time you got your degree, you hadn't seen that gaunt face reflected in the little mirror for nearly two years. While you were at home for a month before reporting for your first job, his mother called and said Richard was sinking. He wanted to see you.

The machine was running faster than you remembered; it labored as it tried to keep up with his need. You sat behind him in the line of his mirror and tried to avoid his sunken eyes. It took a while to decipher his hoarse request; he was insisting on a complete run-down of your prospects. Two summers before, you had successfully avoided subjects which would trigger his envy or self-pity. But on that day, you told all—your plans, the possibility of advancement in your job, your dream of transferring to the overseas division. It seemed to be what he wanted to hear; anyway, you were through playing God. Then he began. You realized quickly how much he had needed your prologue to his story.

"You're planning to live well. I hope and pray you do. I pray a lot now. I pray that I will die well. That's the most important thing I can do, to go out with my head up. Remember what Coach used to tell us about being winners in defeat? He comes to see me almost every week lately and he lets me have it with both barrels. He told me I've got work to do. 'Be strong,' he keeps saying. Being strong is the best that the weak can do. It's their best work. Who learns anything from Superman? They *expect* him to stop a freight train. When I stop a freight train, that's news. I want to make news right here in this cocoon, even if I'm the only one who knows it. See my calendar over there? My Mom marks it for me, but I don't tell her why. Each X is a day when I trusted God. There's a lot more Xs in these last few months. That's good. For three years, I wanted to die every day and thought I'd live in this thing 'til I was 90. Now, they say I've got maybe 90 days, and I know the last one will be the hardest. . . ."

He choked from the effort. His mother came in, turned the machine up a notch, and motioned you out. You walked over to where he could see without the mirror and put your hand on his shoulder. He was smiling as his voice returned: "Don't say you'll see me again. Say something I can believe." You said the only dumb thing you could think of: "Be strong." In the kitchen, his mother was smiling too: "I'm so proud of

Richard. Did you see his calendar, all those Xs? Each one is a victory.'' Even through the closed door, the iron lung sang.

Those who suffer prolonged agony play a most important part in God's plan; they surprise him with trust. The vagaries of the human condition bring them very low, to a place where God would understand their doubt and forgive it. In that nether world of constant pain, the chosen few teach God a lesson, remind him of the reservoir of faith tapped by martyrs to cancer or depression. They ask not for forgiveness but that God might have faith in them. In daily victories over suicide of the spirit, they give their Creator grounds for belief in a race that has caused him infinite disappointment. They are the other Christs who extend and sustain Jesus' witness to human worth. Like Jesus, they redeem the gamble of creation; their valiant struggles make a believer of God and stay his hand one more day.

No one has to tell us what to pray for when we are ill. In the hospital or sick room, healing is the holy grail. For some, however, there comes a day of painful insight. The specialists make their rounds and just happen to drop in when the family is present. Funny how they all arrive at the same time. The prognosis is guarded, the latinisms are elegant, the atmosphere is businesslike. The outline of a new vocation emerges, not all at once, for there is always a period of resistance to bad news. Human nature conspires in a redoubling of petitions for God's mercy until the whole truth sinks in: In spite of the miracles of modern medicine, there will still be unanswered prayers.

Some are called not simply to endure pain, but to suffer, to consecrate pain by faith. The stricken Christian lying amid the glistening, useless machinery of the health industry slowly comes to the conclusion that he or she has been singled out to bear a special burden. After the doctors leave, after the family leaves, one thing remains—the question: "Why me?" Those graced by God eventually discover that the meaning of the choice will be found in prayer. It may take a long time to silence the rasp of bitterness which shatters the voice of God, but he will keep repeating the truth until it is heard. Finally, exhausted by the physical and spiritual struggle, the sufferer gives up the quest for a reasonable explanation and hesitantly begins to contemplate the call. It comes as a shock to hear the Wonder-Counselor, God-Hero, Father-Forever say: "I need you. I need a sign that there is still one person of faith left upon the earth."

All of us are accustomed to turning to God for rescue and protection, but even for the saints among us this new vocation takes some getting used to, for it is nothing less than the ministry of co-redeemer. God asks of the chronically ill a partnership with the suffering Christ who saw no other way to prove to God and to his creation that the gift of being was not given in vain. Living each day in comfort beneath sunny skies proves nothing; living confidently in the endless shadow of pain confirms the rightness of God's plan. Jesus as an octogenarian patriarch could have been the salvation of his immediate family; Jesus on the cross as a young man in his early 30s becomes the hope of the world.

If you have suffered long, pray for more than mere endurance. Pray, instead, to hear the voice hidden deep in your anguish, that gentle word expressing God's need to be glorified in the faith of those broken on the wheel of the world. God did not send you this travail, but now that it has come, he wishes to use you as a light in the darkness. You are called to trust, to let others see a living definition of certainty in his power to save. You are among the chosen who walk with Jesus through the mean streets bearing an unbearable burden. At the end of your journey is hope, hope for the world, hope for God himself. But first, the mean streets.

177

Across the Kidron valley
a grove of ancient olive trees
so dense a man could hide himself
until the storm had passed.

Entwined among the branches
an echo from another time,
an offer welcomed first by Eve
to choose a better way.

You weighed the matter, Jesus,
this finely reasoned argument
against a more exacting course,
and chose your Father's will.

When I would fix on comfort
in place of witness to my faith,
remind me of those gardens, LORD,
and what emerged from each.

From one fled pride far-fallen,
fond hopes, it seemed, forever dashed;
the other poured forth trust-made-flesh
to heal a wounded world.
                    Amen.

Jubilee

And he gave some as apostles, others as prophets, others
as evangelists, others as pastors and teachers, to equip
the holy ones for the work of ministry, for building up
the body of Christ, until we all attain to the unity of faith
and knowledge of the Son of God, to mature manhood,
to the extent of the full stature of Christ, so that we may
no longer be infants, tossed by waves and swept along by
every wind of teaching arising from human trickery,
from their cunning in the interests of deceitful schem-
ing. Rather, living the truth in love, we should grow in
every way into him who is the head, Christ, from whom
the whole body, joined and held together by every supporting ligament, with the proper functioning of each
part, brings about the body's growth and builds itself up
in love (Eph 4:11-16).

    The babble of the crowd was muted by the steel door of the
storeroom. None of those packed into the church basement
knew that the guest of honor was seated on a case of votive lights
taking deep breaths and sweating bullets. He looked up at the
worried pastor, ''I'll be fine in just a minute. It must have been
your sermon, or should I say 'eulogy'? You practically canon-
ized me.'' The younger man smiled, but continued to pace
among the dusty candle stands and leprous statues. This was not
what he had planned at all.

    The old man was well-acquainted with the other occupants
of this room. Over in the corner was black-shrouded Anthony
before whom he had knelt many a time to ask a small favor. Anthony was good for little things. There was dour Vincent de Paul
who had given generous but oh, so solemn assistance to the poor
of the parish. Barely visible was Pius X, robed in a *zamarra* as

white as hosts used to be. They had all been trundled down here in the fever of iconoclasm after the Council. Now they began to spin. He slumped against a tasseled priedieu.

When he came to, a familiar voice was saying something about an ambulance. It was time to speak up, time to stand up. "Clarence Athanasius Townsend. I don't care if you are a doctor now; I am telling you I feel no worse than you did on your wedding day when you fainted at the reception. Did you go to the hospital? No, indeed! You went right on dancing. I'm going to give my little speech. I may even do a step or two myself." Clarence Athanasius reached out to steady him, but he brushed his hands away. "I didn't come back to add to your pay packet."

He had come to celebrate his Fiftieth at St. Christopher's where he had served 37 years. He hadn't wanted all this commotion; it took six months, a sheaf of correspondence, and the pleadings of two hand-picked delegations to deliver him. Although he grumped about all the fuss, he had to admit that the Mass was beautiful, especially the old Latin hymns. Now that the pastor had placed him in the pantheon of saints, the people had received Jesus, and the Bishop had gone back to the Cathedral, it was time to let the old bear out of his cage before Vincent and Anthony and Pius resumed their pirouetting.

The low murmur as he put his shoulder to the heavy door told him the news had been passed around the room. He waved weakly; there were a few gasps, then relieved applause. The podium was sturdy, a blessing from God. He embraced it as he would the Savior.

"You remember me! You laugh, but the memory's the first thing to go. Well, I remember you. When I left here six years ago, I wasn't sure how long you would remain in my memory, but after a little while at the Manor, I realized that's the only way I could have a peaceful retirement: remembering. In fact, the only way for me to get to God lately has been through my memories of you. An old man like me isn't good at thinking of new ways to pray, and when it comes to the tried and true prayers, well, the mind wanders. I go into the chapel with the other old coots and I find I have the attention span of a puppy, until . . . until I think of you.''

He began to call out their names, making each person stand for his brief reminiscence, a phrase or two, too quick for emotion to come to one's face. When they sat down, many covered their eyes. As he remembered God in them, he described God for them: the compassion of God in the practical nurse who spent more time in the homes of the poor than she did in the hospital; the generosity of God in the carpenter who rebuilt the sisters' house after the fire; the creative God in the widow who gave piano lessons to the elderly.

The courage of God was in the three ward leaders who buried the hatchet and stood firm against the bigots. His renewing spirit burned in the unofficial mayor of Old Town who called for the rebirth of the neighborhood after the flood. The God of justice spoke out in the first store owner to stand up to the Machine.

He called out over 40 names. Not all who rose for an instant of celebrity were the persons designated. Many were widows or widowers or children of those who had painted a picture of God as their last work of art. Their survivors stood up for memories of courage and commitment, of selflessness and quiet martyrdom, of the love of God made real by those who had gone before.

The podium squeaked as he leaned more heavily on it. He called out his own name.

''From the vantage point of 50 years, I can finally see just how committed God is to his people. I dare to speak my name because I brought commitment to this parish. Oh, I didn't know it while I was here, but since I retired I began to see how unusual it is for a man to try to do one thing well. When I was active, I was too often caught up with my failures in commitment, but now I see the big picture. I see what it must have meant to you to be able to count on me. Not that I always lived up to your trust, but the basics were there: my Morning Offering, the daily Mass, my regular prayers for you, my presence when bad things happened. I always thought that was small potatoes until I left you in the hands of my successor and started to worry about whether he was always there, always praying. My spies tell me he is, that you are truly blessed. But to get back to me—this is my day, remember—I was not small potatoes. I was there when you needed me. I stand together with all those I have named and all those I didn't have time to name.

"They showed you what God looks like: compassionate, generous, just, patient, life-giving, creative. By the grace of my ordination and the mercy of our God, I showed you what he thinks of you. He is committed to you with no questions asked. Day in and day out, he is with you."

Giving a good talk had always made him glow, but not today; the color didn't return to his face. He stumbled back from the podium even as the doctor and the pastor rose quickly from their chairs behind him. Yet something inside him said he was invincible now, rock-steady, as he swept both hands upward, once, twice. "Please," he said, his voice faltering, "please stand, all of you. I name you, each and all of you, the Church of St. Christopher, the face of God in the Eleventh Ward. And there is one more face of God you have shown me. I can't neglect it and I'm sure many of you have not forgotten it. Time and time again you've shown me that our God is a forgiving God." He blessed them and told them he had to take a ride with Doctor Townsend, "the saintly Athanasius." Then, over his bent shoulder: "But I'll be back for my Sixtieth."

Like all metaphors, that of the church as the body of Christ limps: It is precisely in the limping that we see the glory of the people of God. Unlike the human body, there is no general loss of vigor as individual members wither with age; rather, those who follow are nourished by the sacrifices of their spiritual forebears. An old priest takes his leave by reminding a congregation that his blood is the same as theirs, that he never pretended to be an angel exempt from the longing to see God; their presence recalls for him their needs, the raison d'etre of his vocation. This giving and receiving is the dynamic of the Holy Spirit, the Animator, the Rejuvenator.

Memories of ritual and language, of chant and devotion, bring back to us the way the church was. Our experience of the playing out of life confirms that those days will not come again. But beneath the changes in outward appearance, a different tale is being told, an age-old story of sacrifice and mutual love. This is the story that never ends, a romance about a people who do not merely endure but are born anew with every passing away, a parable of a body alive with the spirit of God, a testament to pilgrims bound for glory.

Prayer for the church can be a very abstract enterprise for the person who sees the church as an entity that hovers just above and outside the limits of human concourse. That is the perfect church that has somehow escaped for two thousand years any contact with the human predicament. Prayer for that church is as frustrating as a campaign to save the unicorns. Neither species exists.

When first we locate the church with our mind's eye, we might picture a great cathedral, a procession of purple capes, a dim figure in white on a high balcony. We may lower our vision to see the humble place of worship at the center of our parish. But with the eye of prayer, we look beyond pomp and edifice and doctrine to gaze upon the faces of our sisters and brothers. There is the real church. There we shall glimpse the face of God.

In praying for the church, we do not forget the divine essence that animates it. After all, our appeals for unity, stability and renewal are directed to the unseen God. Our prayerful hearts, however, soon open to what we know best, to the faces

183

reflecting the needs to which Christ pledged his ministry, the mission of his followers, and, ultimately, his church. The faces in the pews, the faces in the square below the balcony invite our prayer for compassion and understanding, guidance and forgiveness.

Prayer for the faces of the church effects a twofold blessing. First, we hold up to a loving Father the hopes of his children. In our meditation, we see them as individuals—living, breathing, sighing, laughing, weeping members of that part of the human family familiar to us because of the unique roles they play in our personal lives. We know those who gather with us before the altar. We know what blessings they need. We are confident that they will be touched with mercy and love. Second, as we dwell on the faces of our church, we see the characteristics of God living in his people. Their dreams and their sorrows are his. Taken together they form the human face of God two millennia after the apostles looked upon Christ for the last time. A Christian who remembers the church in a daily contemplation on the faces of the faithful will never again complain that God is "out there." He is here, come to life in everyday people.

Pray for the church as you know it in the faces of those who kneel beside you. Pray that they may smile, that in them God will smile upon you.

Five billion plus and counting, LORD,
the facets of your love
spread all around this clouded globe
so perfect from above.
A closer look reveals the faults,
the fissures caused by pride,
the yellow tinge of cowardice,
the stains of sin inside.

Yet you, dear Father, see it all,
the surface and the core,
beholding diamonds in the rough
on which you gently pour
the sacrificial, cleansing blood
that fell from Jesus' cross
to make of this unheeding race
a diadem from dross.
O, send your Holy Spirit now
with hope to clear our sight
that we may see this jeweled earth
reflected in your light.
        Amen.

If Memory Serves

There are times when memory performs a grave disservice. For 300 years, God's chosen people endured the harsh hospitality of the Pharaohs. They prayed for deliverance and God heard their prayers. As cries of anguish rose over the death-riddled homes of their taskmasters, Moses led his people into the night. No sooner did their pursuers' iron-wheeled war chariots begin to rust in the backwash of the Reed Sea, than the newly-liberated thought of trading one kind of slavery for another. So forbidding was the new world of freedom, that they would readily return to the constricting embrace of the Pharaoh if that was the price of security now fondly remembered. "Would that we had died at the LORD's hand in the land of Egypt, as we sat by our fleshpots and ate our fill of bread. But you had to lead us into this desert to make the whole community die of famine!" (Ex 16:3). They were telling Moses that the devil they knew was preferable to the unknown darkness.

There is a nostalgia which enshrines the past at the expense of the future. There are memories which coil around the spirit once filled with hope and drag it backward to hold it captive among embellished yesterdays until death brings release. Such a languid consolation was not the burden of the present work. Here, rather, the recollection of old ways and treasured times was meant to serve the present and illumine the future.

Nostalgia must not become escape. Memories, after having been suitably entertained in the dwelling of consciousness, may implore us to return, to take up a former residence far from this contentious time. If we would continue to call ourselves Christians, we must resist the urge to live in the past.

Our God is the God of the living, not of the dead. He gave us the faculty of memory for insight, for gratitude, for consolation, but never for flight, never for retreat. As we allowed the past to teach us about God, we discovered God where we had not seen him before. We saw his hand in tragedy and triumph; we saw him healing and forgiving, inspiring and comforting; we saw him in the everyday, bringing divine life to ordinary flesh and blood for the sake of a new way of being, for the quickening of his kingdom come and coming. Never once, in any of our reveries, did we see him step back from tomorrow. Whenever we saw the face of God in the mirror of our personal history, it was turned toward the future. All of God's love, all of his power is meant not for yesterday but for what we should be and can be.

As you close this book, recall Jesus' poignant words to Philip at the Last Supper. Philip voiced the yearning of his companions when he asked the Master to "show us the Father, and that will be enough for us." "Philip," Jesus replied, "have I been with you for so long a time and you still do not know me?" (Jn 14:8-9). The solace of our nostalgia lies in our awareness of the repeated revelation of God's action in our lives. Meditation on what he did for us and on where we would be without his saving grace is balm for the soul being pulled to pieces in this frenzied age. Through memories dark and bright we have found that the Father is not hidden from us, that he has described himself as the constant Creator who forms and reforms his people to welcome the future with serenity and courage and hope. He has sent the Holy Spirit of his Son to go ahead of us, to lead us through every passing day.

On that same night in the Upper Room, Peter protested the humiliation of Jesus as he bent to wash the feet of his disciples. In answering, Jesus spoke for his Father, the God whom we have discovered was with us from the beginning: "What I am doing, you do not understand now, but you will understand later" (Jn 13:7). In these pages, we have seen and understood that what has gone before is but a prelude to a new creation. Dag Hammarskjold, the martyred Secretary General of the United Nations (1953-1961), said it best for our day:

If Memory Serves

For all that has been—
    Thanks!
To all that shall be—
    Yes!